LUXOR
AND THE VALLEY
OF THE KINGS

THE AMERICAN UNIVERSITY IN CAIRO PRESS

CONTENTS

TEXT
ALESSANDRO BONGIOANNI

GRAPHIC DESIGN
MARIA CUCCHI

Published in Egypt in 2004 by
The American University in Cairo Press 113 Kasr el Aini Street -
Cairo, Egypt - www.aucpress.com

© 2004 White Star S.r.l.
Via Candido Sassone, 22-24
13100 Vercelli, Italy - www.whitestar.it

This edition published by
arrangement with White Star S.r.l. -
Vercelli, Italy and White Star Egypt L.L.C. -
Sharm El Sheikh, Egypt.

TRANSLATION
AMY CHRISTINE EZRIN

Dar el Kutub No. 14170/03
ISBN 977 424 826 0

Printed in Korea by Doosan Printing
Color separation: Chiaroscuro, Turin

1 *A SPHINX-LINED AVENUE STRETCHES OUT BEFORE THE FIRST PYLON OF THE TEMPLE OF LUXOR.*

2-3 *NEFERTARI, BELOVED BRIDE OF RAMESSES II, WAS PORTRAYED GRACEFULLY IN HER TOMB, IN THE VALLEY OF THE QUEENS.*

4-5 TOP *THE CITY OF LUXOR, SEEN ON THE RIGHT IN THIS VIEW FROM THE SOUTH, WITH ITS TEMPLE IN THE FOREGROUND, IS FLANKED BY WEST THEBES ON THE OPPOSITE SHORE, WHERE THE FUNEREAL MONUMENTS ARE FOUND.*

4-5 BOTTOM *FUNEREAL OFFERINGS FOR MENNA, SCRIBE-PRIEST OF THUTMOSIS IV AND AMENHOTEP III, BURIED IN WEST THEBES.*

6-7 *THIS MAP OF KARNAK, LUXOR, AND WEST THEBES IS TAKEN FROM THE DENKMALER OF RICHARD LEPSIUS, PUBLISHED BETWEEN 1849 AND 1859. THE RELIEFS OF THE TEMPLES ARE OF ITS PRESENT-DAY APPEARANCE.*

8-9 *DEIR AL-BAHARI IS NESTLED AT THE FOOT OF EL-QURNA, THE MOUNTAIN ASSOCIATED WITH THE PRIMORDIAL CHAOS.*

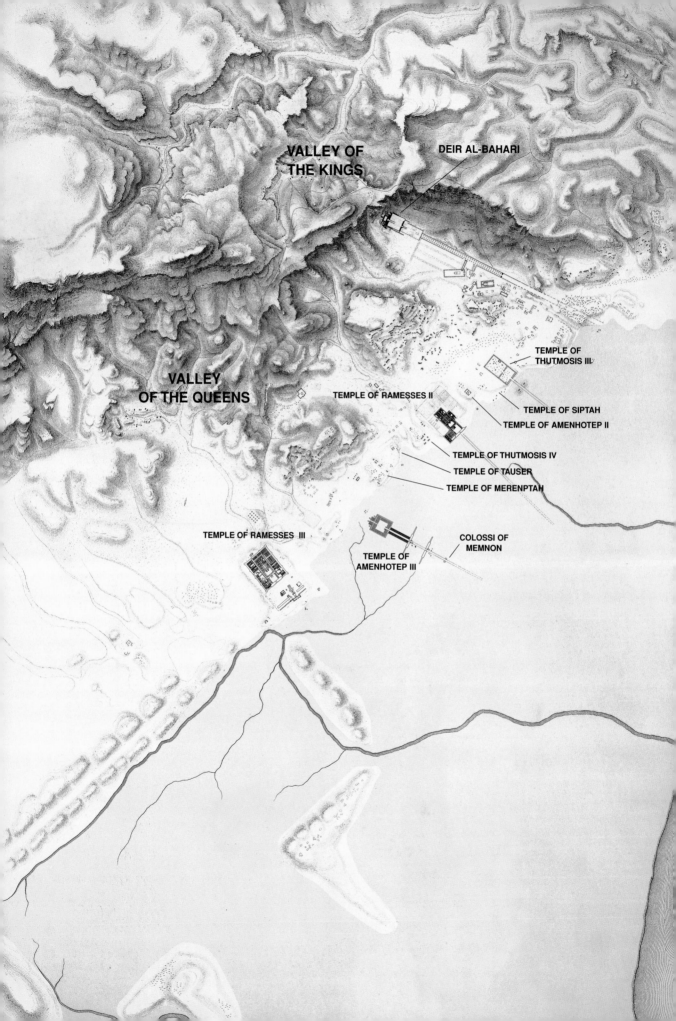

VALLEY OF THE KINGS

DEIR AL-BAHARI

VALLEY OF THE QUEENS

TEMPLE OF RAMESSES II

TEMPLE OF THUTMOSIS III

TEMPLE OF SIPTAH

TEMPLE OF AMENHOTEP II

TEMPLE OF THUTMOSIS IV

TEMPLE OF TAUSER

TEMPLE OF MERENPTAH

TEMPLE OF RAMESSES III

TEMPLE OF AMENHOTEP III

COLOSSI OF MEMNON

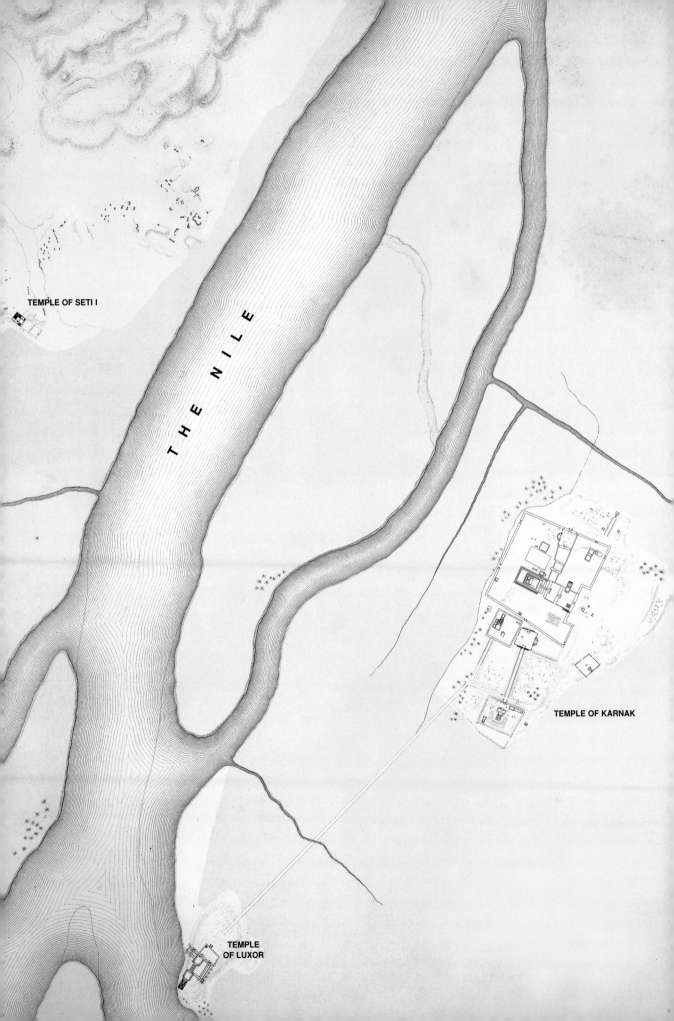

TEMPLE OF SETI I

T H E N I L E

TEMPLE OF KARNAK

TEMPLE
OF LUXOR

PREFACE

"It is believed that, once dawn comes, the base of the colossus and the part that has remained seated on the throne release a sound similar to a cough." Ever since Herodotus (fifth-century B.C.) included this peculiar bit of news in his description of the Colossi of Memnon in West Thebes, the Theban area has rung with an echo that is intriguing, alluring, and mysterious to the peoples of the West, who forever crave "wonders" capable of dispersing the fogs of Europe.

Thebes (or Luxor—it is the City of a Thousand Names), the formidable capital of the Pharaohs of the New Kingdom, whether reigning on the Nile's eastern bank or entombed beyond its western bank, has not ceased since Herodotus' time to attract countless people and fire the imagination with its indescribable appeal.

The city is indescribable because everything is so extraordinary in the region of the Nile's great bend that encompasses the heart of the Two Lands. In the first place, Luxor, east of the river, was the dwelling place of the living and is full of temples, colossi, sphinxes, and obelisks from the early dynasties of the New Kingdom. Rendered gorgeous by the remains of Amenhotep I and Ramesses II's great structures, Thebes (to use the historic name) is the memorial site for Qadesh, the most ancient documented battle in history, and is also the priceless shrine of the ancient Poem of Pentaur. Then, to the west, beyond the Nile, is the Valley of the Kings. Here, the deceased came back to life in the ancient theater of the pharaonic funereal rites that accompanied the sons of the sun god to their appointments with their father and eternity. Thebes is also the place of Howard Carter's far-reaching modern discoveries. Indeed, thanks to an unusual stroke of irony, Carter gave real fame and a palpable presence that overcame a neglect of nearly four millennia to such near-mythical characters as the pharaohs of ancient Egypt.

Carter's discoveries have not, however, led to the loss of any luster. Despite the skepticism and materialism of modern society, it is still possible to imagine the pharaohs as divine. The fame of the sites is such that it seems almost excessive; they are now doubly 'old,' nonrenewable, static—as are their stelae and mummies. However, we are far from any déjà-vus because both sites, to the west and the east of the Nile, continue to be studied, one as much as the other. Many of their monuments have been or are being restored and opened to the public for the first time, while new tombs are regularly uncovered. As the spell that Thebes, Karnak, Luxor, Medinet Habu, and the Valley of the Kings exercise over us is never-ending, the crop of fresh information to be found at these sites is equally copious. These new observations are not at all over dry, too theoretical or uselessly abstract, as the following pages will demonstrate: they deal with human action and divine contemplation, the two most visible and interesting characteristics of ancient Egypt. Indeed, the Land of the Pharaohs is still able to enrich the peoples of the world as it did millennia ago under the leadership of its great monarchs and splendid gods.

---

10 A leopard's head hangs on the chest of the priest Inmutef in this multicolored relief, discovered in the tomb of Ramesses II's father, King Seti I, in the Valley of the Kings.

11 Identified both with a jackal and a dog, Anubis, the god in charge of mummification, is always present in the wall illustrations of Theban necropolises.

LUXOR

ANCIENT THEBES OF THE PHARAOHS

P artly built over the ancient urban layout of Thebes (Uaset for the ancient Egyptians), Luxor's present-day name is derived from the Arabic al-uqsor, or 'the castles,' evoking the castra of the years of Roman rule, as substantiated by the remains of encampments in the temple area. Ancient 'Thebes of a hundred doors,' as the Greeks reflectively named it, was capital of the country during the height of the pharaohs' greatest power. However, absolutely no remains of its original residential settlement have yet turned up; the simple building materials used at the time and the area's continual renovation over successive eras put paid to that hope. The Karnak archaeological area, with the sanctuary of Amun-Ra and the temples of Mut and Montu and the so-called temple of Luxor (once linked together by grandiose avenues of ram-headed sphinxes, the animal manifestation of the god Amun) is where the complex of sacred buildings that, strictly speaking, can be traced back to Thebes, is now found.

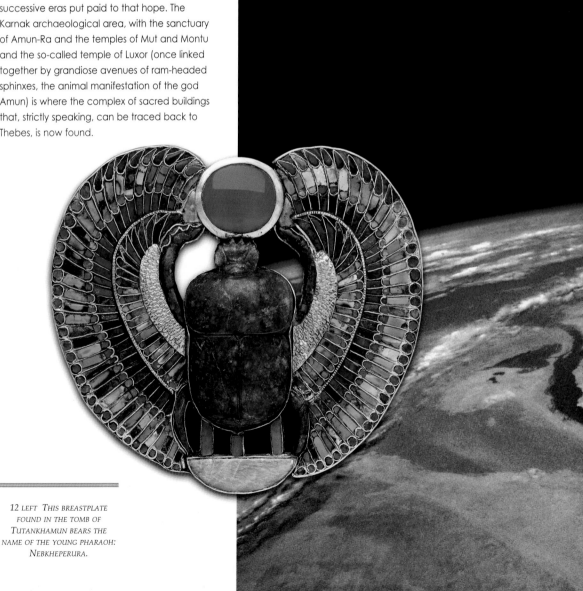

12 LEFT THIS BREASTPLATE FOUND IN THE TOMB OF TUTANKHAMUN BEARS THE NAME OF THE YOUNG PHARAOH: NEBKHEPERURA.

12-13 THE VIEW FROM THE SHUTTLE SHOWS THE ENTIRE COURSE OF THE NILE. THE BEND IN THE RIVER AT LUXOR IS EASILY DISCERNABLE AT THE BOTTOM TO THE RIGHT.

THE TEMPLE OF LUXOR

T he original function of the temple of Luxor appears uncertain. Archaeologists note that the temple must be analyzed in connection with that of Amun-Ra at Karnak, in part because of documented processions held there on sacred holidays. Recent hypotheses suggest that the temple of Luxor, a collection of irregularly developed structures begun during Amenhotep III's reign, then expanded (particularly by Ramesses II), and still further enlarged in later years, should be considered a sanctuary dedicated to the celebration of the royal ka. In other words, the temple would have been the honored site of ceremonies intended to confirm the hereditary principle of the king's sacred power through the attribution of the ka, or the supreme and conceptual legacy passable from father to son.

The early building, which may rest on no longer visible older structures dating back to the Twelfth Dynasty, was the work of Amenhotep, son of Hapu, Pharaoh Amenhotep III's architect and confidant. A brilliant innovator destined to retrace the steps of Imhotep, the famous 'inventor' of the first stepped pyramid at Saqqara, this Amenhotep enjoyed fame and extraordinary power. In fact, he was able to afford his own mortuary temple on the West Theban plan, next to those of the most important pharaohs of the New Kingdom. The temple façade attributed to Amenhotep III (as well as the colonnade, the big courtyard, and the hypostyle hall) was completed and embellished with scenes in relief on the inside walls by the later pharaohs Tutankhamun and Horemheb, who ruled after Akhenaten, pharaoh of a short-lived 'reformed' kingdom. Earlier, Ramesses II's great construction programs led to the building of a vast porticoed courtyard, oddly out of alignment with the axis established

by the other pre-existent buildings. This non-alignment may have resulted from consideration for a small shrine-storehouse dating to the time of Thutmosis.

The new monumental entrance with its massive pylons had walls that originally illustrated Ramesses II's military achievements in the Syro-Palestinian region and against the Hittites. The new entrance featured six colossi, two of which are still located on the side of the gateway; they portray Ramesses II seated next to Queen Nefertari. Of the two obelisks that adorned the entrance, only one remains, since in 1851, Muhammad Ali (Egypt's Turkish ruler) gave the other to Louis Philippe, to be raised in the center of Place de la Concorde in Paris. Beyond the hypostyle hall, whose columns bear the cartouches of Ramesses IV and Ramesses VI, is the vestibule, which during the Roman era was converted into a chapel of the imperial cult and in honor of Serapis.

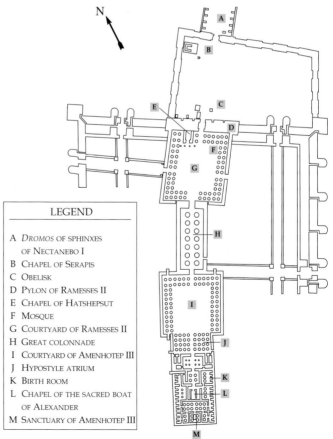

N

LEGEND

A *Dromos* of Nectanebo I
B Chapel of Serapis
C Obelisk
D Pylon of Ramesses II
E Chapel of Hatshepsut
F Mosque
G Courtyard of Ramesses II
H Great colonnade
I Courtyard of Amenhotep III
J Hypostyle atrium
K Birth room
L Chapel of the sacred boat of Alexander
M Sanctuary of Amenhotep III

Alexander the Great rebuilt the temple's sanctuary in the form of a chapel. In Amenhotep III's time the sanctuary had been intended to shelter the sacred boats, but later its inside and outside walls portrayed Alexander as a pharaoh, making offerings to the Ancient Egyptian gods, with his own name in the appropriate cartouche. These decorations are a rare and important record that proves the immense significance of the Macedonian monarch's brief stay on Egyptian soil. Near the sanctuary, another decorated space of great importance is found: the hall of the theogony, or 'sacred birth,' of Pharaoh Amenhotep III.

To legitimize his rule, Amenhotep III chose to portray

16 AND 17 TOP TWO COLOSSI PORTRAYING RAMESSES II AND TWO OBELISKS (ONE IS FOUND TODAY IN PLACE DE LA CONCORDE IN PARIS) WERE SITUATED IN FRONT OF THE FIRST PYLON OF THE TEMPLE.

17 BOTTOM A SPHINX-LINED AVENUE LINKED THE TEMPLE OF LUXOR WITH THAT OF KARNAK IN ANCIENT TIMES.

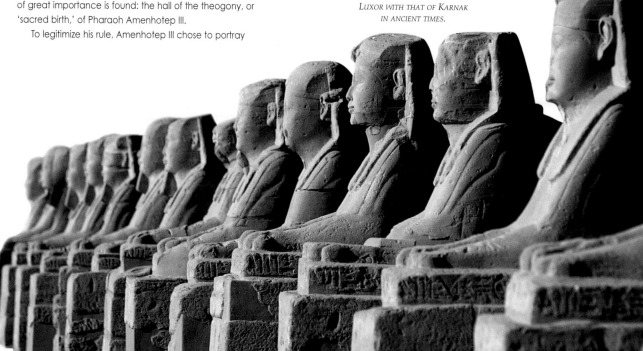

himself in a series of reliefs emphasizing his conception of a divine origin, as Hatshepsut had done before him on the walls of her own mortuary temple at Deir al-Bahari. A few years ago, during reinforcement work on the structures, a series of statues of extraordinary artistic quality portraying gods and New-Kingdom pharaohs came to the light in Amenhotep's porticoed courtyard. The effigies were located in a ditch inside the temple intended to safeguard the 'deposed' but yet still sacred images, the heritage of an entire community. Today, these fascinating sculptures can be admired in the underground halls of the Luxor Museum.

18

18 TOP AT THE BASE OF THE OBELISK STILL ON SITE, FOUR BABOONS ARE DEPICTED, VENERATED ANIMALS CONSIDERED SACRED.

18 BOTTOM LEFT THE SURVIVING OBELISK STANDS OUTSIDE THE MONUMENTAL PYLON OF RAMESSES II.

18 BOTTOM RIGHT ON THE OBELISK, THE NAMES OF RAMESSES II ARE REPEATED SEVERAL TIMES.

19 IN THIS PHOTO, THE FIRST PYLON OF THE TEMPLE OF LUXOR AND THE OBELISK CAN BE DISTINGUISHED, CONSTRUCTED ACCORDING TO THE WILL OF RAMESSES II.

THE TEMPLE OF LUXOR

22 *ON THE BELT AND PLEATED
KILT OF THIS COLOSSUS SITUATED
INSIDE THE TEMPLE OF LUXOR,
THE NAME OF THE CELEBRATED
RAMESSES II IS RECORDED.*

23 *THIS DETAIL OF THE FACE OF
ONE OF THE COLOSSAL STATUES IN
THE COURTYARD OF RAMESSES II
IN THE TEMPLE OF LUXOR
REVEALS THE CALM AND
PEACEFUL EXPRESSION OF THE
LONG-LIVED PHARAOH.*

*20-21 AND 20 BOTTOM THE
LARGE COURTYARD OF RAMSES II
IS CHARACTERIZED BY A SERIES OF
COLOSSI PORTRAYING THE LONG-
LIVED PHARAOH, WHO DIED IN HIS
EIGHTIES.*

*21 RIGHT AT THE SIDES OF THE
THRONE OF ONE OF THE COLOSSI
OF RAMESSES II, THE NILE
DIVINITIES PERSONIFYING UPPER
AND LOWER EGYPT ARE
PORTRAYED, A CUSTOMARY
CHARACTERISTIC OF ROYAL
STATUARY.*

THE TEMPLE OF LUXOR

24 *The temple of Luxor seen from the southwest: between the big colonnade, visible in the foreground, and the first pylon, in the background, stands the mosque of Abu al-Haggag, built in the fourteenth century.*

25 *top and center The courtyard of Amenhotep III, an Eighteenth-Dynasty pharaoh, is supported by 64 fascicled columns.*

25 *bottom As was customary in ancient Egypt, the temples were embellished with numerous statuary groups portraying pharaohs and gods. It was also expected of kings to usurp monuments dedicated to their predecessors.*

26 TOP ON THE WALLS OF THE TEMPLE, NUMEROUS SCENES OF OFFERINGS TO THE GODS ARE DEPICTED IN RELIEF.

26-27 RAMESSES II PRESENTS OFFERINGS TO THE THEBAN TRIAD (AMUN-RA, MUT, AND KHONSU).

27 TOP IN THIS PHOTOGRAPH, THE ELEGANT FASCICLED COLUMNS WITH THE CHARACTERISTIC PAPYRUS FORM, WHICH LINE THE SO-CALLED 'COURTYARD OF AMENHOTEP III,' CAN BE ADMIRED.

27 BOTTOM IN THIS RELIEF, A PHARAOH WEARING THE BLUE CROWN HOLDS A SCEPTER AND A FLAIL, UNMISTAKABLE SYMBOLS OF WARLIKE QUALITIES AND POWER.

28 Even though the cartouches claim that the pharaoh portrayed here is Horemheb, the delicate lines almost surely belong to the young Tutankhamun.

29 The temple of Luxor is characterized by a few chapels decorated with numerous reliefs, such as that at the top to the right showing a sacred procession, or that at the bottom immortalizing the pharaoh by illustrating him with the god Ra-Harakhty, intent on offering him the key of life.

THE LUXOR MUSEUM

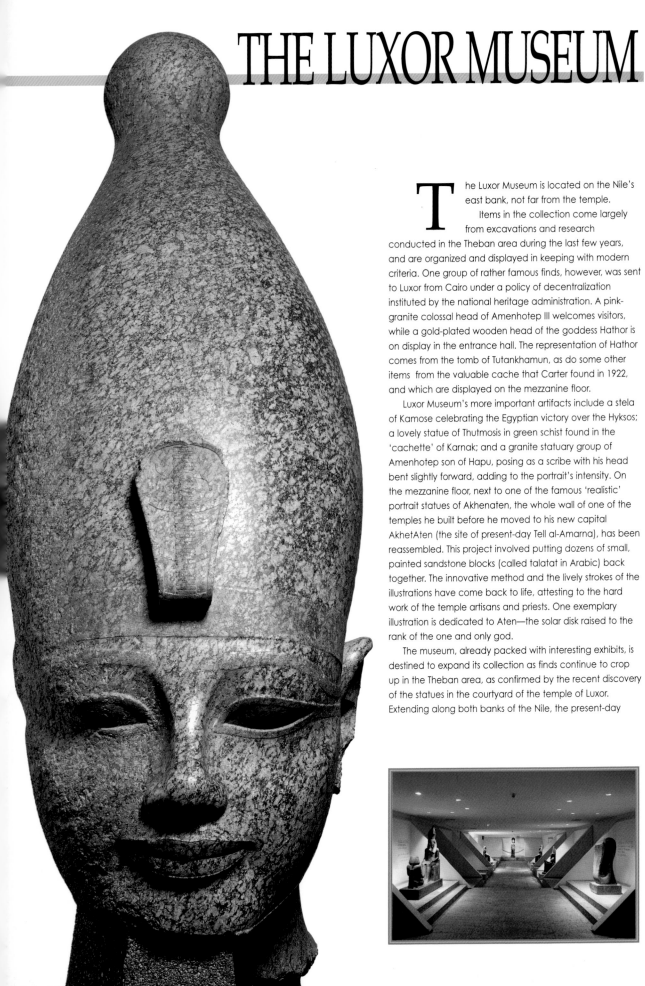

The Luxor Museum is located on the Nile's east bank, not far from the temple.

Items in the collection come largely from excavations and research conducted in the Theban area during the last few years, and are organized and displayed in keeping with modern criteria. One group of rather famous finds, however, was sent to Luxor from Cairo under a policy of decentralization instituted by the national heritage administration. A pink-granite colossal head of Amenhotep III welcomes visitors, while a gold-plated wooden head of the goddess Hathor is on display in the entrance hall. The representation of Hathor comes from the tomb of Tutankhamun, as do some other items from the valuable cache that Carter found in 1922, and which are displayed on the mezzanine floor.

Luxor Museum's more important artifacts include a stela of Kamose celebrating the Egyptian victory over the Hyksos; a lovely statue of Thutmosis in green schist found in the 'cachette' of Karnak; and a granite statuary group of Amenhotep son of Hapu, posing as a scribe with his head bent slightly forward, adding to the portrait's intensity. On the mezzanine floor, next to one of the famous 'realistic' portrait statues of Akhenaten, the whole wall of one of the temples he built before he moved to his new capital AkhetAten (the site of present-day Tell al-Amarna), has been reassembled. This project involved putting dozens of small, painted sandstone blocks (called talatat in Arabic) back together. The innovative method and the lively strokes of the illustrations have come back to life, attesting to the hard work of the temple artisans and priests. One exemplary illustration is dedicated to Aten—the solar disk raised to the rank of the one and only god.

The museum, already packed with interesting exhibits, is destined to expand its collection as finds continue to crop up in the Theban area, as confirmed by the recent discovery of the statues in the courtyard of the temple of Luxor. Extending along both banks of the Nile, the present-day

*30 LEFT AMENHOTEP III,
PORTRAYED HERE, LIVED DURING
THE EIGHTEENTH DYNASTY.*

*30 RIGHT THE MUSEUM OF
LUXOR (THE MAIN HALL IS
SHOWN HERE) IS MODERN AND
USER-FRIENDLY.*

*31 LEFT SOME MASTERPIECES
ARE FOUND OUTSIDE THE
MUSEUM, SUCH AS THIS
COLOSSUS OF THUTMOSIS III.*

*31 RIGHT THIS COW'S HEAD
COMES FROM THE TREASURE OF
TUTANKHAMUN.*

town has undergone noticeable structural
development in the last few years. Luxor of the
past was a picturesque village that over the
centuries had grown up around the remains of
the temple; later it was enriched by colonial
buildings that fitted perfectly into the local
environment. Luxor of the present is a shining blaze of myriad
little souvenir shops, standing near large hotels on the
eastern bank of the Nile. To experience the real nature of
the town and its inhabitants, the visitor must move away
from the river, into the narrow alleys of the center or the
market, where it is still possible to breathe in the exotic
atmosphere that has long attracted travelers from around
the world. Luxor of course remains an indispensable
destination for all visitors to this part of Egypt because of its
geographical centrality and the rich archaeological remains
it guards.

32 LEFT THIS MARCHING STATUE OF AMUN WAS FOUND IN THE TEMPLE OF KARNAK.

32 TOP RIGHT THE KING HOREMHEB KNEELS BEFORE THE GOD ATUM IN THIS STATUARY GROUP FOUND IN THE TEMPLE OF LUXOR.

32 BOTTOM RIGHT CONSIDERED A MASTERPIECE OF ANCIENT EGYPTIAN STATUARY, THIS EFFIGY OF THUTMOSIS III WAS DISCOVERED IN 1904 AT KARNAK.

33 THE GODDESS HATHOR, HERE CROWNED WITH A SOLAR DISK, HOLDS AN ANKH, THE SYMBOL OF LIFE, IN HER RIGHT HAND.

34 *The unmistakable profile of the heretic pharaoh Akhenaten is reproduced in this colossal statue.*

35 TOP *This small model boat comes from the funereal cache of Tutankhamun.*

35 CENTER RIGHT *The small wooden statue plated with gold leaf found in the tomb of the young Tutankhamun probably portrays the young Eighteenth-Dynasty king.*

35 BOTTOM *This alabaster sphinx was most likely sculpted for Tutankhamun.*

*36 LEFT THE GODDESS
SEKHMET, THE DIVINITY WITH
THE ASPECTS OF A LIONESS, IS
PORTRAYED IN THIS
MAGNIFICENT GRANITE STATUE.*

*36 RIGHT ISIS EMBRACES THE
SOVEREIGN IN A SIGN OF
PROTECTION IN THIS DAMAGED
STATUARY GROUP, SCULPTED IN
ALABASTER.*

*37 IN THIS EXTRAORDINARY
SCULPTURE IN ALABASTER, OR
BETTER IN CALCITE, THE GOD
SOBEK, WITH THE ASPECTS OF A
CROCODILE, PROTECTS THE
PHARAOH.*

THE TEMPLE OF KARNAK

38 *IN FRONT OF THE EIGHTH PYLON OF THE TEMPLE OF KARNAK, THREE SEATED COLOSSAL STATUES ARE LOCATED WEST OF THE ENTRANCE.*

39 *THE PHOTO CLEARLY SHOWS, IN THE FOREGROUND, THE SECOND PYLON AND THE BIG HYPOSTYLE HALL OF THE TEMPLE OF KARNAK.*

The Karnak archaeological area includes three temple complexes encircled by unfinished brick-wall enclosures. The temples within are dedicated to the god Amun-Ra, the goddess Mut, and the god Montu, respectively. The great temple of Amun, the main divinity of Thebes from at least the Twelfth Dynasty on, is the sanctuary par excellence of the whole New Kingdom, of the Theban dynasties at the height of their glory. The Twelfth Dynasty is also the period to which the area's earliest documented sacred buildings (today completely vanished) can be dated.

Almost all the pharaohs, from Thutmosis I (beginning of the Eighteenth Dynasty), to Amenhotep III, Ramesses II and III, until those of the Twenty-second Dynasty, contributed to the construction or enlargement of the numerous spaces that were added along the approach to the temple's original nucleus.

While standing before the grandiose pylons (tapering block structures) probably built by Nectanebo I and II and the first Ptolemys at the entrance, and before entering the temple's large interior courtyard, it is useful to note the presence of a platform, or landing stage. Here boats tied up that sailed along the canals linking the various temples used during the solemn holidays in honor of the gods. Inside the first courtyard, featuring porticoes along its northern and southern sides with columns topped by cluster-bud papyrus capitals, stand several tall sacred buildings. Among them, to the left, is a small temple dedicated by Seti II to the Theban triad composed of Amun, Mut, and Khonsu. Both the statues, of colossal proportions and originally situated at the entrance of this little temple, are today outside Egypt. One is at the Louvre, Paris; the other is in the Egyptian Museum, Turin.

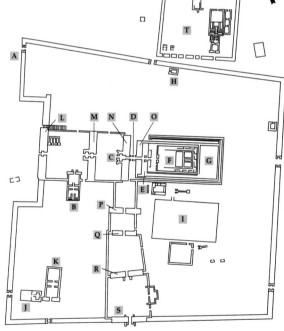

LEGEND

A	ENCLOSURE OF AMUN	K	TEMPLE OF KHONSU
B	TEMPLE OF RAMESSES II	L	FIRST PYLON (OF NECTANEBO)
C	BIG HYPOSTYLE HALL	M	SECOND PYLON
D	OBELISK	N	THIRD PYLON
E	*UAGIT* (SMALL HYPOSTYLE HALL)	O	FOURTH PYLON
		P	SEVENTH PYLON
F	MIDDLE-KINGDOM COURTYARD	Q	EIGHTH PYLON
G	*AKH-MENU*	R	NINTH PYLON
H	TEMPLE OF PTAH	S	TENTH PYLON
I	SACRED LAKE	T	TEMPLE OF MONTU

40 *TOP THE BIG COURTYARD OF THE TEMPLE IS DOMINATED BY A 69-FOOT-TALL COLUMN, THE ONLY SURVIVING ONE OF AN ANCIENT KIOSK.*

40 *BOTTOM AND* 40-41 *AN AVENUE LINED BY CRIOSPHINXES (WITH A RAM'S HEAD) UNRAVELS BEFORE THE FIRST PYLON OF THE TEMPLE.*

41 *TOP CRIOSPHINXES STAND IN A ROW IN THE BIG COURTYARD OF THE TEMPLE OF KARNAK.*

On the right side of the courtyard, inserted into the so-called Portico of Bubastis (named after the Nile delta city from which the Twenty-second Dynasty rulers originated), is the important temple of Ramesses III. It may have been used for the solemn celebration of the important sed Festival, or Royal Jubilee, marking the 30th anniversary of a pharaoh's accession to the throne. A row of Osirid pillars decorates the temple's first courtyard, while the wall illustrations depict a procession in honor of the god Min. A small ramp gives access to the hypostyle hall and the sanctuary of the boat of Amun, which is flanked by two smaller chapels for the boats of Mut and Khonsu. At the center of the courtyard, the imposing gazebo of Taharqa (Twenty-fifth Dynasty) rises, with columns more than 66 feet tall (today only one remains).

The second pylon, preceded by a pair of colossal statues of Ramesses II, leads to the big hypostyle hall with its 134 giant-sized columns. The central nave, elevated above the other rows of columns, features large window openings at the top, designed to illuminate the interior. The second pylon was commissioned by Pharaoh Horemheb, and made abundant use of recycled materials, above all from Akhenaten's time; but the twelve columns of the central nave were raised by Amenhotep III. The interior decoration of the hypostyle hall, begun by Ramesses I, was mostly completed by Seti I and Ramesses II. It features scenes of prayer and offerings to the gods, as was the habit in spaces where only priests and those authorized by the cult were permitted to enter.

In contrast, the hypostyle hall's outside walls commemorate the military virtues of the two great Nineteenth-Dynasty pharaohs: Seti I, shown on his military campaigns in Syria and Palestine and on those against the Libyans, and Ramesses II in his epic battle at Qadesh against the Hittites.

THE TEMPLE OF KARNAK

43 TOP THIS UNUSUAL PERSPECTIVE DRAWS ATTENTION TO THE BIG COURTYARD OF THE TEMPLE OF KARNAK WITH THE SECOND PYLON AND THE ENTRANCE TO THE HYPOSTYLE HALL.

43 BOTTOM THE TEMPLE OF RAMESSES III, ON THE RIGHT OF THE BIG COURTYARD, IS CHARACTERIZED BY OSIRID PILLARS PORTRAYING THE PHARAOH.

The third pylon, erected by Amenhotep III, used to hide hundreds of filler blocks taken from a series of buildings that had been dismantled. (Two of these, the 'white chapel' of Senusret I and the alabaster one of Amenhotep I were rebuilt in a private area north of the first courtyard.) On the internal façade of the third pylon, which is rather dilapidated compared to the complex's other structures, a valuable relief decoration was found showing the young Amenhotep IV in the traditional scene of 'massacring the prisoners' before Amun. This is the proof that, in the first years of his reign, even the future Akhenaten led military campaigns against the enemies of Egypt, thus contradicting his fame as an all-out pacifist.

A courtyard built by Thutmosis I but decorated by Thutmosis IV, in which four obelisks were also found originally, leads to the fourth pylon, which served as an entrance to the New Kingdom's oldest temple. In the vestibule created between the fourth and fifth pylons are statues representing the pharaoh dressed in the typical outfit of the sed Festival and a nearly 100-foot-tall obelisk in red granite from Aswan, raised by Queen Hatshepsut on the occasion of her own sed Festival. On the faces of the sixth pylon, besides the fragments of the 'Annals' of Thutmosis III, a summary and record of the pharaoh's numerous military campaigns in the East and the names of the cities and peoples subjugated by the Egyptians, appears; they are enclosed within a kind of 'fortress-cartouche.'

The sanctuary of the sacred boats contains many interesting decorations, among which a scene that depicts moving the barge of Userhat stands out. Opposite and around this building, in a maze of small spaces that were reconstructed several times, the two red-sandstone statues of Amun and Amunet, attributed to Tutankhamun, are worth

43

noting. In addition, there is a section of the 'Annals' of Thutmosis III, with a list of the war booty set aside as donations to the temple of Amon at Karnak.

A vast spread-out courtyard is all that remains of the primitive, Middle-Kingdom-temple nucleus. A French archaeological mission to the area over the last few years was able to complete a survey of the zone and also a study of the finds that have been made.

The so-called 'party hall,' or Akh-menu, of Thutmosis III, found on the other side of the Middle-Kingdom courtyard, is a peristyle building with 32 pillars and 10 columns. It was probably used for celebrating the sed Festival, on each sovereign's 30-year anniversary as ruler. Many rooms surrounding the main hall contain important historical and artistic information. Among them are the famous 'Chamber of the Ancestors,' a relief (now in the Louvre) in which Thutmosis II makes offerings before 57 of his predecessors, and the 'Botanical Garden,' whose wall illustrations of partly real and partly make-believe exotic plants and animals constitute a unique document about the Egyptians' knowledge of the world at the time of Thutmosis III (ca. 1504-1450 B.C.).

Many other buildings are located in the area adjacent to the main body of the temple of Amun; some have been excavated, others remain to be investigated. The mysterious 'expressionist' statues of Akhenaten that were found just beyond the perimeter enclosure wall made it possible to identify the location of the first buildings dedicated to Aten, those dedicated while Akhenaten still lived in Thebes. The expansion of the big temple of Amun to the south included four more pylons. They start with the pylons Thutmosis II and III erected and end with that of Horemheb, who helped himself to ample amounts of materials (talatat) used in the construction of the temples of Aten as filler for his own structures. Today, the thousands of recycled talatat sit in a sort of 'open-air' museum not far away.

44 TOP AND BOTTOM ON THE COLUMNS OF THE HYPOSTYLE HALL AT KARNAK, RAMESSES II IS PORTRAYED INTENT ON PRESENTING OFFERINGS TO VARIOUS DIVINITIES.

44-45 THE HYPOSTYLE HALL BUILT BY RAMESSES II IS A TRUE ARCHITECTURAL MASTERPIECE.

45 TOP EVEN THE WALLS OF THE HYPOSTYLE HALL FEATURE NUMEROUS RELIEFS, SUCH AS THIS ONE IN WHICH THE PHARAOH IS REVERED BY SOME GODS.

THE TEMPLE OF KARNAK

Not to be missed in a visit to the main complex of the sanctuary of Amun are the sacred lake dating to the time of Pharaoh Taharqa, used exclusively for the ritual boat trips specified in the local liturgical calendar, and the lovely example of a cella temple. This temple, dedicated by Ramesses II to Khonsu, was decorated by the priest-king Herihor (among others); he is shown dressed as a pharaoh, with his name enclosed in a cartouche.

Two more enclosed buildings, dedicated respectively to the goddess Mut and the god Montu, stand in the area of Karnak. The temple of Montu, in rather poor condition and still under excavation, honors the oldest god of the Theban region, who was only later unseated by Amun, soon to become the dynastic and national god. Built by Amenhotep III, the building was connected by a series of canals to the other temple of Montu at Medamud, a place that, together with Tod and Ermonti, was a particularly important site within the Theban district for the worship of this god's cult. In the vast area dedicated to Mut—largely unexplored as yet—beyond a large, irregularly-shaped sacred lake, a temple used by the goddess' cult and two smaller temples are found, one dedicated to Amun-Ra built by Amenhotep III, and the other built by Ramesses III. All the structures are quite dilapidated and await restoration and reinforcement. Lastly, it is important to recall that the many statues portraying the goddess Sekhmet (given her possible assimilation with Mut) exhibited in various European collections in fact come from the temple of Mut at Karnak. All the effigies in question (about 300 works in all) were sculpted at the time of Amenhotep III and, according to a recent interpretation, they constituted, thanks to the formulas engraved on them, an actual "stone liturgy whose true meaning still eludes us."

46 AND 47 THE RELIEFS ON THE WALLS OF THE TEMPLE OF KARNAK HAVE PROVIDED SCHOLARS WITH MUCH INFORMATION ABOUT THE HISTORY OF AND EVENTS IN ANCIENT EGYPT. THE ELEVATED STYLISTIC LEVEL REACHED BY THE ARTISANS WORKING ON THE TEMPLE OVER THE CENTURIES CAN ALSO BE NOTICED IN THE IMAGES. IN PARTICULAR, ON THE BOTTOM TO THE LEFT, RAMESSES II CAN BE SEEN KNEELING BEFORE A PERSEA TREE AS HE RECEIVES ABUNDANT PRAISE FROM AMUN-RA. ON THE BOTTOM TO THE RIGHT, PORTERS BEARING THE SACRED BOAT OF AMUN-RA ARE PORTRAYED: THEY ARE ACTUALLY PRIESTS DRESSED UP WITH JACKAL'S HEADS.

48 *Photographed from a dizzying perspective, the two obelisks erected by Thutmosis I and Queen Hatshepsut stand at the center of the temple complex of Amun.*

49 TOP *Osirid pillars graced many of the temple's courtyards.*

49 CENTER *The god Thoth, with the head of an ibis, is easily recognizable in this painted high relief found in the chapel of Hatshepsut.*

49 BOTTOM *This statue with delicate features portrays the god Amun-Ra, one of the main divinities worshiped in the temple of Karnak.*

50-51 *The temple of Karnak underwent numerous additions over the course of thirteen centuries of history, and its various structures reveal diverse stylistic influences, such as the pillars featuring the symbols of Upper and Lower Egypt (top left) dating back to the time of Thutmosis III, the Osirid pillars, and the late-epoch entrance (right).*

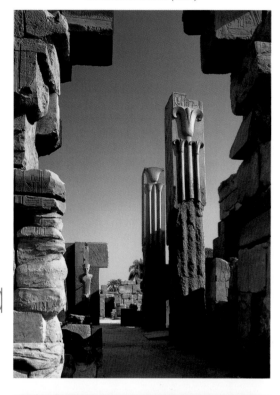

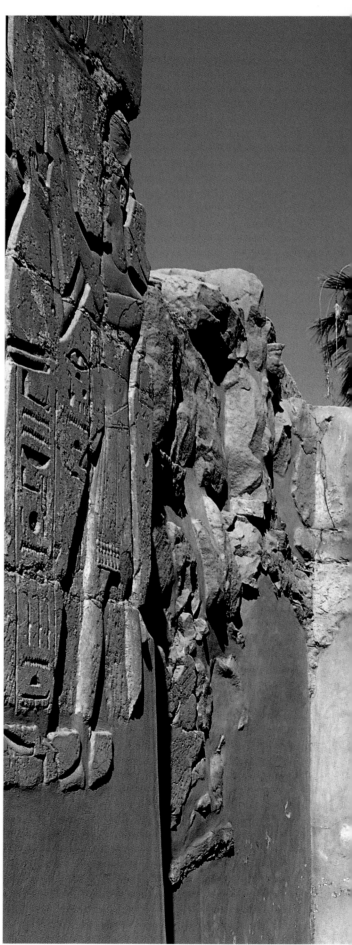

THE TEMPLE
OF KARNAK

53 TOP LEFT SETI I IS PORTRAYED
IN THE ACT OF STRIKING HIS ENEMIES.

53 TOP RIGHT IN THIS
BAS-RELIEF, SCENES OF OFFERINGS
TO THE GODS CAN BE ADMIRED.

54-55 IN THIS AERIAL VIEW, THE
FIRST PYLON IS IN THE
FOREGROUND.

MORTUARY

I n an attempt to avoid the ravages of time and to ensure for themselves the kind of immortality that their religious beliefs allowed them, Egyptian kings had, in every era, the considerable privilege and duty to prepare for themselves tombs as rich as possible and suitable to their rank. During the Old Kingdom (2686-2181 B.C.), a pharaoh's last resting place came to take on a regular pyramidal form, which included a place of worship annexed to the actual burial spot, forming a single entity. However, during the New Kingdom, there was a preference to separate the worship area from that specifically devoted to entombment.

At the beginning of the Eighteenth Dynasty (1569-1293), the pharaohs ruling from Thebes (on the Nile's eastern bank, today known as Luxor) chose the part of the Libyan range that from the natural formation known as the Theban Peak (Qurn in Arabic) overlooks the whole Theban plain. There they cut their hypogeums (underground tombs) deep into the rock. However, on the narrow strip of land on the Nile's western bank that runs between the border of the cultivated area and the first slopes of the Theban range, they erected their so-called mortuary temples. These sacred buildings, only partially preserved today, are more or less aligned with the land of West Thebes and maintain an ideal connection to their related crypts, often aligned on the same axis.

Queen Hatshepsut (ca. 1498-1483 B.C.) provided a striking and especially admirable example of this custom. First she had her mortuary temple built in the most perfect and evocative natural setting, one with the rosy glow of a rock wall for a background and with the temple's ramps and colonnades easily seen in the distance. Then she had her tomb cut into the opposite face of the mountain, in what is called the Valley of the Kings. Her "pharaoh's" tomb complex (so-called since Hatshepsut already possessed a tomb in a small valley not far away, built when she had not yet assumed royal prerogatives), culminated, after a uniquely awkward and winding route, in the sarcophagus chamber. This was situated right at the back of the very same underlying wall of her own mortuary temple.

56-57 THE AERIAL PHOTOGRAPH ENCOMPASSES THE WHOLE AREA OCCUPIED BY MONUMENTS BUILT EXPRESSLY FOR THE FUNERAL RITES OF THE PHARAOHS.

LEGEND
A TEMPLE OF RAMESSES III AT MEDINET HABU
B TEMPLE OF AY-HOREMHEB
C TEMPLE OF THUTMOSIS II
D TEMPLE OF AMENHOTEP III AND COLOSSUS OF MEMNON
E TEMPLE OF AMENHOTEP, SON OF HAPU
F TEMPLE OF THUTMOSIS I
G TEMPLE OF MERENPTAH
H TEMPLE OF TAUSERT
I TEMPLE OF THUTMOSIS IV
J TEMPLE OF RAMESSES II, RAMESSEUM
K TEMPLE OF AMENHOTEP II
L TEMPLE OF SIPTAH
M TEMPLE OF THUTMOSIS III
N TEMPLES OF MENTUHOTEP, THUTMOSIS III, HATSHEPSUT, DEIR AL-BAHRI
O TEMPLE OF SETI I

TEMPLES

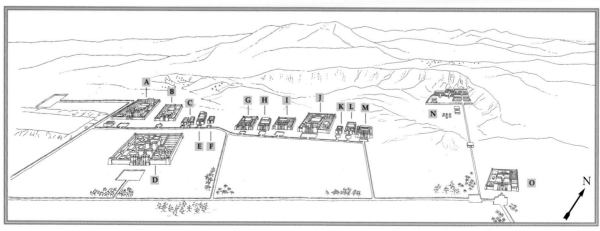

THE TEMPLE OF

T he architect Senenmut drew inspiration from the most direct and ancient typological precedent from the Eleventh Dynasty (ca. 2040-1972 B.C.), one that stands right next to Hatshepsut's temple complex. Senenmut certainly knew how to introduce conceptual innovations, while borrowing architectural elements already tested many times elsewhere, and he succeeded in creating a masterpiece destined to preclude even pale imitations. A unique monument of unrepeatable beauty, Hatshepsut's temple complex fully exploits the resources of the natural environment, into which it seems inserted almost like a theatrical backdrop. A high squared rock wall stands out majestically, enclosing the many terraces of which the complex is composed, but which unfortunately have not survived fully intact.

Perhaps it was no coincidence that Hatshepsut, to whom many cultural and religious ideas are attributed that bore fruit following the reforms of Akhenaten, the 'heretic pharaoh' who ruled from 1350 to 1334 B.C., chose to erect her mortuary temple right here. The complex was directly supported by a rear wall and did not use structures cut into

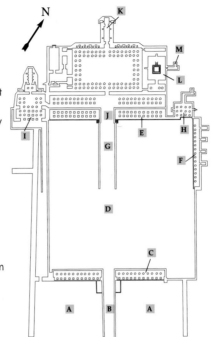

LEGEND
A FIRST COURTYARD
B RAMP
C LOWER PORTICO
D SECOND COURTYARD
E CENTRAL COURTYARD
F NORTHERN PORTICO
G SECOND RAMP
H LOWER CHAPEL OF ANUBIS
I CHAPEL OF HATHOR
J UPPER PORTICO
K CHAPEL DEDICATED TO THE ROYAL FAMILY AND AMUN
L COURTYARD DEDICATED TO THE CULT OF THE SUN OF RA-HARAKHTY
M UPPER CHAPEL OF ANUBIS

58 bottom This head of an Osirid pillar, today in the Cairo Museum, portrays Hatshepsut.

59 The temple complex of Deir al-Bahri was built with the mountain at its back.

the rock. There was a succession of vast terraces, partly given over to gardens, linked by wide ramps. The complex was endowed with a courtyard with a simple altar on the upper terrace in the place of a pyramid or obelisk (as was the rule in the Fifth Dynasty sun temples). In all, the complex, with its splendid and unique shape, was a product of Senenmut's genius. To this man, Queen Hatshepsut's architect and confidant, goes the credit of knowing how to invent new solutions, never used again because of reasons of political opportunism, since Hatshepsut saw herself condemned to a sort of damnatio memoriae, influencing even the artistic relationships that she had promoted.

Hatshepsut's successors returned to the practice of constructing their mortuary temples on the West Theban plain. Perhaps only the Nubian temples of Ramesses II (1279-1212), particularly that at Abu Simbel, revived at least some of Senenmut's legacy of ideas. This legacy infused the great rock temples facing onto the Nile with some of that vital, vibrant projection resulting from a communion with nature that appears to have reached it height at Deir al-Bahri.

THE TEMPLE
OF HATSHEPSUT

*62-63 AND 62 BOTTOM ALL THE
COLUMNS ON THE SECOND
TERRACE WERE ADORNED WITH
MUMMIFORM SANDSTONE
STATUES CONNECTED WITH
OSIRIS, GOD OF THE AFTERLIFE.*

*63 BOTTOM LEFT IN THE
CHAPELS OF THE TEMPLE,
NUMEROUS PAINTED RELIEFS CAN
STILL BE ADMIRED.*

*63 BOTTOM RIGHT THE GOD
HORUS, PORTRAYED HERE,
WEARS THE DOUBLE CROWN OF
UPPER AND LOWER EGYPT.*

THE TEMPLE OF

*64-65 AND 65 TOP THE TWO
COLOSSI OF AMENHOTEP III
WERE FOUND IN FRONT OF THE
FIRST PYLON OF THE FUNERAL
TEMPLE DEDICATED TO THE CULT
OF THE PHARAOH.*

*64 BOTTOM THIS STUCCO HEAD
PORTRAYING AMENHOTEP III IS
FOUND TODAY IN THE EGYPTIAN
MUSEUM, CAIRO.*

AMENHOTEP III

T he monumental mortuary temple of Amenhotep III (1410-1372 B.C.) is the work of his influential architect Amenhotep, son of Hapu, already the author of many other sacred buildings in Thebes that later earned him deification like his distant predecessor Imhotep, the famed architect-physician. Of Amenhotep's complex, only the two colossi, known as the Colossi of Memnon, have survived. These two huge statues, which portray the pharaoh seated in the traditional hieratic position, are 53 feet tall (in addition to the 8-foot base). They originally flanked the entrance to the temple, whose vastness can only be imagined, as nothing of the two architectural structures has survived. Among the few finds recovered is a sandstone stela inscribed with the act by which Amenhotep III consecrated the temple to Amun. The Greek geographer Strabo records that in 27 B.C. an earthquake seriously damaged the colossus standing to the north, opening a crack in the stone up to the belt. This 'wound' gave rise to the legend that at either dawn or at the first puff of wind the statue would 'sing,' as happened in the case of the god Memnon, when the Greeks saluted his mother Aurora. Attracted by the fame of the 'colossi' of Thebes, numerous Greek and Roman travelers left behind accounts of their visits; their comments and epigrams were in evidence as early as A.D. 120, when Emperor Hadrian visited the area. The comprehensive restoration that Emperor Septimius Severus (193-211) ordered abruptly interrupted the 'gift for singing' of Amenhotep III and his colossus.

LEGEND

A COLOSSI OF MEMNON
B FIRST PYLON
C SECOND PYLON
D THIRD PYLON
E SOLAR COURTYARD
F ENCLOSURE WALL

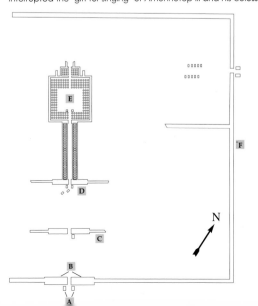

N

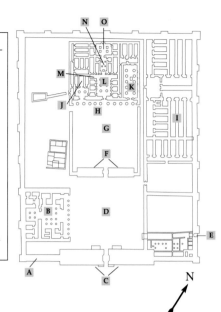

LEGEND

A ENCLOSURE WALL
B ROYAL PALACE
C FIRST PYLON
D FIRST COURTYARD
E NORTHERN ENTRANCE
F SECOND PYLON
G SECOND COURTYARD
H PORTICO
I STOREHOUSES
J ROOM OF RAMESSES I
K SOLAR COURTYARD
L HYPOSTYLE HALL
M TRANSVERSE CORRIDOR
N SANCTUARY OF AMUN-RA
O FOUR-PILLARED ROOM

Near the village of Qurna rises the temple of Seti I, of which only the central part, starting from the hypostyle hall, has been relatively well preserved, revealing interesting, quality decorations. Preceded by two pylons in bare brick, today almost entirely deteriorated or gone, the surviving spaces recall a tripartition that suggests internal rooms dedicated respectively to Amun and Seti I (center), Amun and Ramesses I (south), and Amun-Ra (north). The presence of a chamber dedicated to the cult of the Seti's father, Ramesses I, who occupied the throne for only two years, further demonstrates Seti's filial piety. As already shown in the case of the tombs in the Valley of the Kings, Seti wanted to complete what had been planned for his short-lived predecessor, whose cult and commemorative worship he wished to ensure.

66 BOTTOM THIS ALABASTER STATUE OF SETI I, DISCOVERED IN A HIDING PLACE IN THE TEMPLE OF KARNAK, IS FOUND TODAY IN THE EGYPTIAN MUSEUM, CAIRO.

67 IN THIS AERIAL VIEW, THE VARIOUS AREAS THAT CONSTITUTE THE TEMPLE COMPLEX CAN BE BETTER OBSERVED.

68 THESE PAPYRIFORM COLUMNS ARE LOCATED INSIDE THE HYPOSTYLE HALL OF THE TEMPLE.

69 TOP THE WALLS OF THE HYPOSTYLE HALL, LIKE OTHER AREAS IN THE TEMPLE, ARE COVERED WITH BAS-RELIEFS DEDICATED TO THE CULT OF THE PHARAOH AND SOME GODS.

69 BOTTOM IN THE FIRST COURTYARD OF THE TEMPLE, A FEW VOTIVE STELAS PORTRAYING SETI I CAN BE SEEN.

The hypostyle hall with its six papyriform columns features scenes of of Seti I and his son and successor Ramesses II making offerings to Amun and the Ennead. Ramesses II in turn, worked on completing construction of the sacred buildings, which included a so-called 'royal palace,' the first of its kind found in the area, intended to accommodate the 'revived' defunct king on important holidays. The presence of a small paved basin in the temple's largest area may refer to the cosmogonic event. This is the emergence of the primordial hill, as described in the so-called Osireion of Abydos, the mysterious building annexed to the big temple begun by Seti I and completed by Ramesses II in the sacred city of the god Osiris.

The mortuary temple of Ramesses II (1304-1337 B.C.) is a splendid complex of buildings that replicates his father Seti I's temple while enlarging it and enriching it with many wall decorations. It had already become famous at the time of the Greek geographer Strabo and his near contemporary the historian Diodorus Siculus, as well attested to in written sources. Named the Ramesseum by Jean-François Champollion (1790-1832), the pioneer decipherer of hieroglyphics, who was fascinated by the place and left behind a precise description, the temple of Ramesses II today still projects grandiosity, despite its decay. The Ramesseum is surrounded by an external wall and a series of big warehouses built of bare brick as are the ceiling vaults; these are among the few examples of curvilinear construction in Egypt, where such typology both in the floorplan and elevated areas was shunned. In its main structure, the Ramesseum has two pylons and two courtyards, leading to various hypostyle halls. The inner façade of the first pylon, which is extremely damaged, shows battle scenes between the peoples of the Near East and in particular the Hittites, with a depiction of the famous battle of Qadesh. The epic encounter, which took place on the banks of the Orontes River, in the Syro-Palestinian region, was also reproduced in buildings in Karnak, Abydos, and above all at Abu Simbel. At

RAMESSES II

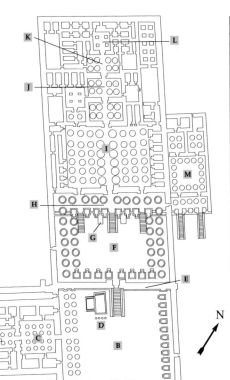

LEGEND

A FIRST PYLON
B FIRST COURTYARD
C ROYAL PALACE AND PRIVATE APARTMENTS
D COLOSSUS OF RAMESSES II
E SECOND PYLON
F SECOND COURTYARD
G STATUE OF 'YOUNG MEMNON'
H GALLERY OF THE VESTIBULE
I BIG HYPOSTYLE HALL
J ASTRONOMIC ROOM OR 'ROOM OF THE BOATS'
K ROOM OF THE LITANIES
L SANCTUARY
M *MAMMISI*-TEMPLE OF TUY AND NEFERTARI

70-71 SEEN HERE FROM THE SOUTH, THE FUNERAL TEMPLE DEDICATED TO RAMESSES II, OR THE RAMESSEUM, APPEARS IN ALL ITS VASTNESS.

71 THIS UPPER PORTION OF A COLOSSUS OF RAMESSES II IS CONSERVED AT THE BRITISH MUSEUM.

this last site, the depiction was even accompanied by a record of events, known today as the 'Poem of Pentaur,' from the name of the scribe who drafted it. In the first courtyard, which is bordered by a double row of columns and Osirid pillars, is a seated colossus of Ramesses now in fragments (intact it would be over 56 feet in height). The hypostyle hall, which appears elevated with respect to the level of the courtyards, presents splendid examples of columns with campaniform and papyriform capitals. On the walls, in addition to the customary images of military campaigns in Asia, there appears a procession of Ramesses' sons and daughters, from the oldest to the youngest.

THE TEMPLE OF RAMESSES II

72 THE HYPOSTYLE HALL AND THE SECOND COURTYARD OF THE TEMPLE ARE CLEARLY RECOGNIZABLE IN THIS PHOTO.

73 TOP OSIRID COLOSSI PORTRAYING THE PHARAOH ARE SET AGAINST PILLARS DELIMITING THE SECOND COURTYARD.

73 BOTTOM TRACES OF COLOR ARE STILL PRESENT ON THE COLUMNS OF THE HYPOSTYLE HALL, THUS REVEALING, EVEN IF ONLY PARTIALLY, THE ANCIENT SPLENDOR OF THE TEMPLE.

74-75 AND 74 BOTTOM TODAY COMPLETELY COLLAPSED, A COLOSSUS OF TRULY IMPRESSIVE SIZE (ABOUT 56 FEET TALL) WAS LOCATED IN THE FIRST COURTYARD OF THE TEMPLE.

75 BOTTOM LEFT THIS FRAGMENT PROBABLY FELL FROM A SEATED STATUE OF RAMESSES.

75 BOTTOM RIGHT THE GOD AMUN-RA, ACCOMPANIED BY THE GODDESS MUT, HANDS THE ATTRIBUTES (FLAIL, SCEPTER, AND SWORD) TO RAMESSES II THAT WILL GUARANTEE HIM A LONG REIGN.

76-77 IN THIS RELIEF, THE GOD RA-HARAKHTY HANDS THE ANKH, SYMBOL OF LIFE, TO THE PHARAOH.

THE TEMPLE
OF RAMESSES II

THE TEMPLE
OF RAMESSES II

*78-79 TOP RAMESSES II, ABOARD
HIS CHARIOT, IS PORTRAYED
IN THE ACT OF SHOOTING
AN ARROW.*

*78 BOTTOM LEFT IN THIS SCENE,
RAMESSES II RECEIVES THE ATEF-
CROWN FROM AMUN-RA,
ESCORTED BY MUT.*

*78-79 BOTTOM SOME OF
RAMESSES II'S CHILDREN WALK
BEFORE A SACRIFICIAL BULL.*

THE TEMPLE OF

The great archaeological complex of Medinet Habu (the 'city of Habu,' an Arab place name of uncertain origin) encompasses numerous buildings of various ages. It is surrounded by a thick wall in bare brick, the majority of which dates back to the time of Ramesses III (1198-1166 B.C.). The oldest evidence found here demonstrates that Ramesses III chose a site specially dedicated to Amun as the place to erect his own mortuary temple. He wanted to create in his own undying memory a group of commemorative religious edifices that would be rivaled in grandeur in the Theban area only by those of Karnak. The great temple of Ramesses III is fronted by a royal pavilion, or rather a large monumental gate carved out of

the wall enclosure, which was inspired by the nearby Asian fortresses that the king had encountered during his military campaigns. The square construction in bare brick, today largely lost, included two towers, originally more than 66 feet tall. Inside is a kind of passageway that becomes continuously narrower toward the end, on the walls of which appear scenes of devotion to the gods, such as Amun, Seth, or Maat, in addition to a rich repertoire of images of prisoners personifying peoples the pharaoh had conquered. The great temple of Ramesses III, which is modeled on the Ramesseum, with its two porticoed courtyards, three hypostyle halls, and a sacred boat sanctuary, all surrounded by chapels (some intended to store rich offerings to Amun), is in nearly excellent condition.

RAMESSES III

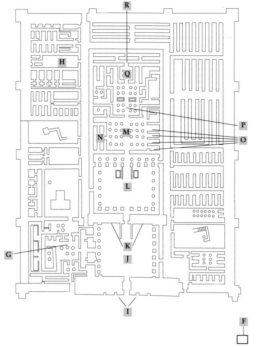

LEGEND

A ENTRANCE
B MIGDOL
C CHAPEL OF THE DIVINE ADORATRICES
D TEMPLE OF THE EIGHTEENTH DYNASTY
E SACRED LAKE
F NILOMETER
G ROYAL PALACE
H STOREROOMS
I FIRST PYLON
J FIRST COURTYARD
K SECOND PYLON
L SECOND COURTYARD
M BIG HYPOSTYLE HALL
N ROOMS OF THE ROYAL TREASURE
O CHAPELS DEDICATED TO VARIOUS DIVINITIES
    AND THE DIVINE RAMESSES III
P SECOND HYPOSTYLE HALL
Q THIRD HYPOSTYLE HALL
R CHAPEL OF RAMESSES III

N

81

80-81 IN THIS AERIAL VIEW OF
THE TEMPLE DEDICATED TO
RAMESSES III, THE FIRST PYLON
CAN BE SEEN IN THE
FOREGROUND.

81 BOTTOM LEFT LIBYAN ENEMIES
DEFEATED BY RAMESSES III ARE
PORTRAYED IN THIS RELIEF.

81 BOTTOM RIGHT THIS STATUE
OF RAMESSES III, TODAY AT THE
EGYPTIAN MUSEUM, WAS FOUND
IN A HIDING PLACE IN THE
TEMPLE OF KARNAK.

The first pylon's façade depicts the customary scenes of the pharaoh sacrificing prisoners before Amun and also presents a long list of conquered nations, among them the so-called 'Peoples of the Sea.' These tried to disembark in the Nile Delta but were repelled, as the inscriptions and reliefs on the temple's external walls confirm. On the internal wall of the first pylon, Ramesses III is in the presence of his protector deities, at the head of his army while he massacres his enemies and celebrates his victory by flaunting hands and chopped-off members and heaping up piles of his adversaries. On the back wall, to the left of the first courtyard, the royal palace from which the pharaoh could attend ceremonies was entered through the 'Window of Appearances.'

The second pylon, preceded by an elegant ramp, also bears a variety of descriptions of the king's military undertakings, gives onto a second porticoed courtyard decorated with religious scenes and processions of the divine boat. In the big hypostyle hall, there remain only the truncated shafts of 24 columns that had originally supported the ceiling.

On the external walls, on the southwest side, hunting scenes and the important religious festivals are depicted, while on the northeast side, the famous scenes of naval battles against the Libyans can be admired.

In the district of Medinet Habu there is a temple dating back to the beginning of the Eighteenth Dynasty, as the cartouches of Amenhotep I and Thutmosis I confirm. Completed later on, it was endowed with a monumental entranceway by Ptolemy XV (44-31 B.C.), while the Roman Emperor Antoninus Pius (A.D. 138-161) had a courtyard and fore-buildings constructed. The internal and external decorations of the sanctuary and peristyle record the names of many of the most famous pharaohs of the New Kingdom, from Thutmosis III to Horemheb, from Seti I to Amenmesse, while the decorations on the doors date back to the Ptolemaic era.

82 LEFT THE PORTICO OF NECTANEBO I, IN THE SMALL TEMPLE OF AMUN, WAS SUPPORTED BY POLYLOBATE BELL-SHAPED CAPITALS.

82 BOTTOM RIGHT THIS PYLON, DATING BACK TO THE TWENTY-FIFTH DYNASTY, WAS ERECTED BY THE PHARAOH TAHARQA.

83 THE FIRST AND SECOND PYLONS OF THE TEMPLE, OF WHICH THE ENTRANCES ARE VISIBLE, ARE COVERED WITH RELIEFS.

THE TEMPLE
OF RAMESSES III

84 TOP LEFT THE PORTICO ENCLOSING THE SECOND COURTYARD STILL FEATURES PAVING STONES REMAINING ALMOST INTACT.

84 TOP RIGHT MANY RELIEFS SHOW RAMESSES III AS HE DOMINATES HIS ENEMIES.

84-85 FEW REMAINS OF OSIRID PILLARS ARE FOUND ON THE COLUMNS OF THE SECOND COURTYARD.

85 TOP A BATTLE SCENE IS FEATURED IN THIS RELIEF.

85 RIGHT THIS STATUE PORTRAYING SEKHMET IS INSIDE THE TEMPLE.

86-87 THIS GROUP OF PRISONERS IS ILLUSTRATED ON THE WEST SIDE, ON THE OUTSIDE OF THE SECOND PYLON.

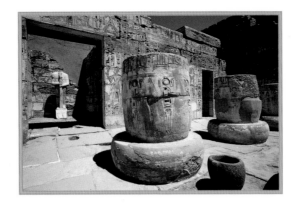

89 TOP OF THE TWO HYPOSTYLE
HALLS, ONLY THE BASES OF THE
COLUMNS REMAIN.

89 BOTTOM IN THIS RELIEF, THE
PHARAOH PRESENTS AND
RECEIVES OFFERINGS FROM
THE GODS.

90 TOP TRACES OF THE ORIGINAL COLORS CAN STILL BE SEEN IN THE RELIEFS ON THE PORTICO.

90 BOTTOM THE DECORATIONS OF THE TEMPLE MAKE IT POSSIBLE TO EXPAND OUR KNOWLEDGE OF THE HISTORY OF RAMESSES III.

91 PAPYRIFORM COLUMNS STILL BEARING TRACES OF COLOR CHARACTERIZE THE PORTICO OF THE SECOND COURTYARD.

92-93 ON BACK OF THE SECOND PYLON, RAMESSES III IS PORTRAYED ON HIS CHARIOT AS HE HUNTS THE SACRED BULL.

THE VALLEY OF THE KINGS

I n the bowels of the mountain, among deserted and silent valleys, a hard-working community of laborers and artisans cut into the rock, preparing vast walls. On them were sculpted, incised, or painted the beautiful figures of men, gods, and animals, the protagonists in the complex mythological-religious world that Egyptians believed inhabited the afterlife. These deep cavities, splendidly decorated, led directly to the presence of the pharaoh, whose mummified cadaver was to be found within a heavy sarcophagus of stone in the pillared room that is the sole end-point on the route to these burial places. They even awoke the wonder of ancient Greek travelers. "Above the Memnonium are found, in certain caves dug into the rock, about 40 tombs of kings, marvelous works that deserve to be seen." These words of the Greek geographer Strabo, who in about 25 B.C. visited the place now universally known as the Valley of the Kings (from the Arabic Biban al-Muluk), found confirmation in the descriptions of later writers. The Greek historian-topographer Pausanias, who in the second century A.D. ventured into this rich burial grounds of kings, followed the narrow lines of access into the living rock, called them 'pipes,' or syrinx in Greek, a term which came to him spontaneously, recalling the tubes of a flute. Many tombs in the Valley of the Kings had already been entered, pillaged, and had suffered all kinds of violations since their excavation in the pharaonic era. The tombs later became ideal refuges for Christians who dedicated themselves, in solitary confinement, to meditation and prayer during the faith's expansion into Egypt in the third century A.D. These impassioned new inhabitants caused major damage and, following their departure, the royal necropolises sank over the

centuries into complete abandon, prey to bandits and looters. The first Westerners to extract precious 'scientific' evidence from the ancient sites were the savants that Napoleon brought with him on his expedition to Egypt in 1799. These men, driven by anxiety for knowledge, retraced (not only metaphorically) the fascinating valley's steep paths: they also succeeded in discovering the tomb of Amenhotep III in the adjacent valley to the west. It was the only royal tomb, other than that of King Ay, to be found in this region.

Texts and images on the walls of the royal tombs of the New Kingdom (1569-1081 B.C.), as in the truly extraordinary case of the Seti I's tomb, do not have a descriptive or commemorative purposes. They are rather intended to reproduce, or better yet 'recreate,' through the repertory taken from the abundant literary and iconographic work of a sepulchral nature—the so-called Books of the Lower World—a suitable environment for the otherworldly voyage of the deceased. The wall decoration takes its inspiration (when it does not reproduce the exact formula, changing only the proportions), from the 'Books' which also existed on papyrus. The wall decoration does not seek to be only an artistic testimony—though this essential quality must be recognized—but is an indispensable aid in the process of the god-king's rebirth.

In the case of Seti I and his splendid tomb, the decorative plan provided for an arrangement of texts and figures fitted to the architectural structure. This arrangement occurred within a layout that reflected the utmost respect for the king and that was constant through to the last Ramesside pharaohs (end of the Twentieth Dynasty). In the

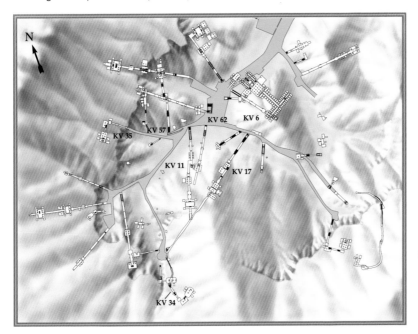

LEGEND	
KV 6	RAMESSES IX
KV 11	RAMESSES III
KV 17	SETI I
KV 34	THUTMOSIS III
KV 35	AMENHOTEP II
KV 57	HOREMHEB
KV 62	TUTANKHAMUN

94-95 THE VALLEY OF THE KINGS WAS PROBABLY CHOSEN AS A ROYAL BURIAL SITE BECAUSE IT IS OVERLOOKED BY A PYRAMID-SHAPED MOUNTAIN.

long entrance corridors, texts and images from the Litany of the Sun are encountered. They are a sort of introduction for the deceased ruler (as well as for the modern visitor) to the complex world of the afterlife, populated by numerous gods and demons. Among these first-seen formulas and depictions are the 75 qualities and manifestations of the sun god (the ancient Egyptian Ra) whom the king must meet before he can unite with him. Farther down the corridor, and beyond the sarcophagus chamber, appears the famous Book of He Who Is in the Netherworld, known to Egyptologists by the name of Book of the Amduat. This book can be considered an account of the voyage and encounters that the sun god completes in the underworld, over the course of the twelve hours of the night. It is also the key to understanding the architectural structure of the burial place. After considering the religious apprehensions that are assuaged in the Book of the Amduat, a German scholar has recently formulated an interesting new hypothesis about the well sunk along the route to the royal tomb. The author states that the well, like every room and corridor of the tomb, had a precise religious function. It was not dug to

defend the tomb against desecrators or to avoid the possible infiltration of water, as thought until now, but was dug simply because it belonged to the religious scheme on which the layout of the tomb was based. The Book of Gates, a work analogous to the Book of the Amduat by virtue of its content, describes the dangerous voyage, fraught with obstacles—the 'doors' of the title, which the king must know how to face and then pass through. In this text, the rooms found beyond the one in which the well was dug appear decorated, whereas the walls of the room with the well show scenes of what can be defined generically as adoration of and offerings to the gods. In the last section of the corridor that links the tomb complex's first rooms with the actual crypt, or rather the sarcophagus chamber, are found other reproductions of the Book of Gates, and illustrations and formulas relating to the 'Opening of the Mouth' ritual are outlined. In the New Kingdom, in connection with this process, rites and magic practices are noted as being in the power of the priests, initiated in the sacred science. They alone have the ability to return the deceased to life, therefore assuring them eternal existence.

THE TOMB

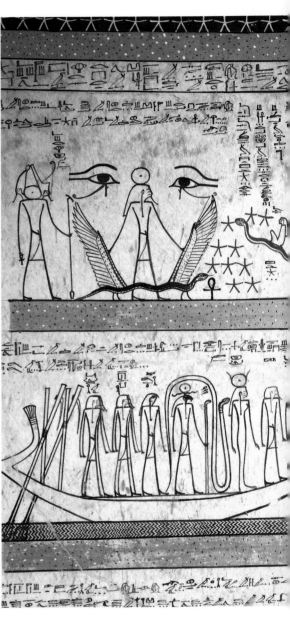

The tomb of Thutmosis III (1504-1450 B.C.), among the most illustrious and powerful pharaohs in ancient Egypt's history, is at the end of the Valley of the Kings in a narrow gorge about 100 feet below ground; it is reachable today by an iron staircase. The tomb, which was among the first to be excavated in the valley, has a hairpin-turn pathway, as was common during the Eighteenth Dynasty. From this pathway, a steep corridor leads down, across two small spaces and past a deep well, to a first chamber with pillars decorated with images of divinities traced in paint. A staircase at the end gives access to the actual burial chamber, in the shape of a big cartouche, thus repeating the established model of the hypogeums dug in the valley for Thutmosis I. These however, consisted in a single space that was not even decorated. In the case of Thutmosis III, the walls of the burial chamber, painted with a white background in imitation of a single, huge, unrolled papyrus, appear completely covered with hieroglyphic inscriptions and sketched figures, both stylized and decisively original. The text and the illustrations that appear here present the famous Book of the Amduat ('He Who Is in the Netherworld'), that collection of magical-religious formulas, knowledge of which allows the deceased to overcome the obstacles in the course of his nocturnal voyage. The latter unfolds across a period that corresponds to the twelve hours of the night; it is carefully scheduled and reflects the topography of the mortuary temple and also the sun's nocturnal course. Thutmosis III's sarcophagus was found inside the burial chamber: it was empty, with its cover in pieces on the ground. In fact, in 1898, almost 20 years before the opening of Thutmosis' tomb, Victor Loret had found the king's mummy at Deir al-Bahari, where many royal mummies had been hidden.

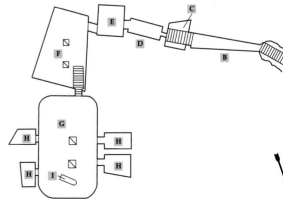

LEGEND

A Entrance
B First corridor
C First room
D Second corridor
E Well
F Upper room with pillars
G Funereal chamber
H Side chambers for
   offerings
I Sarcophagus

96 top The ceiling of the tomb features a starry sky.

96 center On the walls of the funereal chamber, the twelve hours of the night of the Amduat are portrayed.

96-97 and 97 bottom In the two registers, some of the stages in the Amduat, the text recounting the nighttime voyage of the pharaoh in the netherworld, are illustrated. On the bottom of the walls, some of the 741 gods in the Amduat are portrayed.

THE TOMB OF THUTMOSIS III

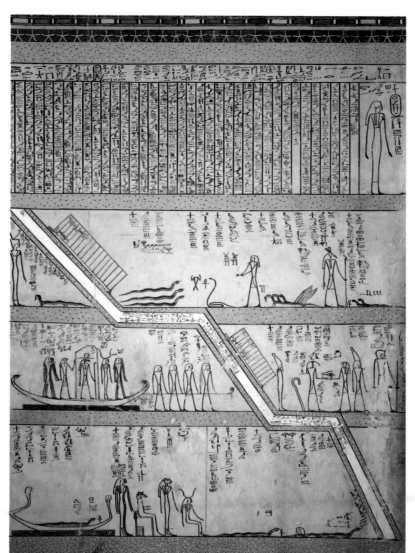

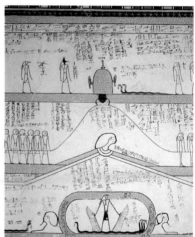

98 *TWO PILLARS CHARACTERIZE THE FUNEREAL CHAMBER IN THE TOMB OF THUTMOSIS III.*

99 TOP LEFT *THE BOOK OF THE AMDUAT IS ILLUSTRATED ON THE WALLS OF THE TOMB, DIVIDED INTO FOUR REGISTERS.*

99 BOTTOM LEFT *IN THIS DETAIL, THE ACCURACY OF THE DECORATION ON THE SARCOPHAGUS OF THUTMOSIS III CAN BE ADMIRED.*

99 TOP RIGHT *IN THE PHOTO, SOME FIGURES FROM THE LITANIES OF RA REPRODUCED ON ONE OF THE PILLARS IN THE FUNEREAL CHAMBERS CAN BE SEEN.*

99 BOTTOM RIGHT *IN THIS PHOTOGRAPH, THE TEXTS FROM THE FIFTH AND SIXTH HOURS OF THE AMDUAT CAN BE SEEN. THE GOD SOKAR IS PORTRAYED IN THE OVAL.*

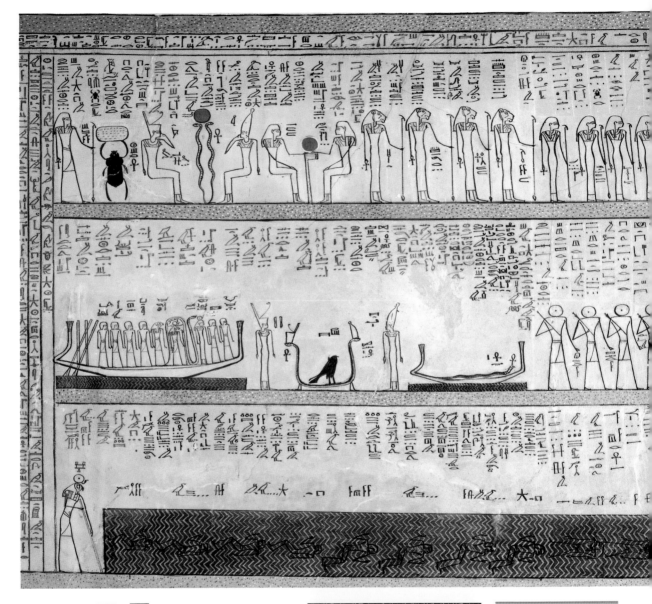

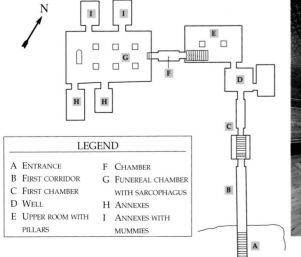

LEGEND

A ENTRANCE
B FIRST CORRIDOR
C FIRST CHAMBER
D WELL
E UPPER ROOM WITH
   PILLARS
F CHAMBER
G FUNEREAL CHAMBER
   WITH SARCOPHAGUS
H ANNEXES
I ANNEXES WITH
   MUMMIES

*100-101 THE SCENES ON THE
WALLS OF THE TOMB, WHICH
REFER TO THE AMDUAT, WERE
PAINTED USING ONLY RED AND
BLACK.*

*100 BOTTOM THE FUNEREAL
CHAMBER OF AMENHOTEP II IS
CHARACTERIZED BY SIX PILLARS
DECORATED ON ALL FOUR OF
THEIR SIDES.*

*101 RIGHT ON ONE OF THE
PILLARS, THE GOD OSIRIS IS
PORTRAYED IN THE ACT OF
HANDING THE ANKH, THE
SYMBOL OF LIFE, TO THE
PHARAOH.*

AMENHOTEP II

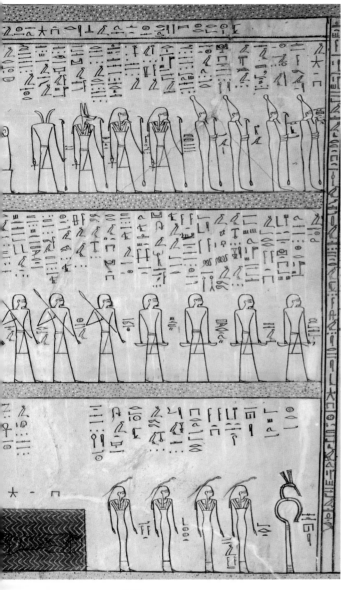

T he tomb of Amenhotep II (1454-1419 B.C.), Thutmosis III's son and successor, was discovered by Loret in 1898. In structure and decoration, it closely resembles his father's tomb, with an analogous sequence of two corridors and a well leading to an initial pillared room from which, through a walled entrance, an even larger burial chamber is entered. The walls are painted in imitation of papyrus and decorated with texts and illustrations from the Book of the Amduat, while the pharaoh accompanied by various divinities appears on the pillars. Amenhotep's burial chamber abandons the oval cartouche shape found in the tombs of the Thutmosis I, II, and III, revealing a star-filled ceiling with a blue background. At the back of this last room of the tomb, a red-painted sandstone sarcophagus was found; it contained the still intact mummy of

Amenhotep II, wearing a mimosa necklace. Why the tomb robbers had spared the earthly remains of the king, normally dressed with jewels and with precious amulets hidden among the bandages with which the corpse was wrapped, remains unknown. Further, in the tomb of Amenhotep II (more precisely, in a side annex), another nine royal sarcophagi with the mummies of Thutmosis IV, Amenhotep III, Merenptah, Seti II, Siptah, Sethnakht, Ramesses IV, Ramesses V, and Ramesses VI were discovered. It was probably during Pinedjem I's reign, at the beginning of the Twenty-first Dynasty (ca. 1070-1030 B.C.), that in order to protect the mummies from further violation, their relocation to the hiding place at Deir al-Bahari was ordered. Today, most of the royal bodies found at West Thebes are conserved in the Egyptian Museum in Cairo, which exhibits only a small part of the collection in a separate and private hall.

102 AND 103 TOP LEFT AND RIGHT AMONG THE VARIOUS DIVINITIES PORTRAYED ON THE SARCOPHAGUS OF AMENHOTEP II, ISIS KNEELING ON THE SYMBOL FOR GOLD, ANUBIS WITH HIS UNMISTAKABLE JACKAL'S HEAD, AND TWO UDJAT EYESCAN BE DISTINGUISHED ON THE LEFT.

103 BOTTOM TO THE LEFT OF THE ENTRANCE TO THE FUNEREAL CHAMBER OF AMENHOTEP II'S TOMB, SOME COBRAS ALSO CALLED URAEI CAN BE NOTICED IN THE LOWER REGISTER.

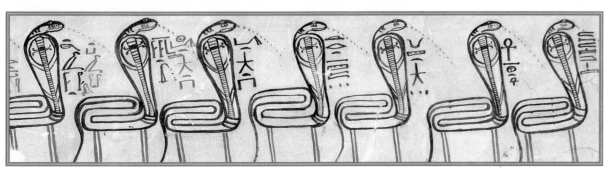

THE TOMB

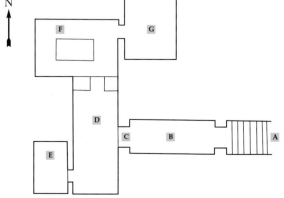

OF TUTANKHAMUN

The tomb that Howard Carter discovered in November 1922, just below the entrance to the tomb of Ramesses VI, revealed the name Tutankhamun. This pharaoh died very young and in never clearly understood circumstances; more significantly, he introduced the world to funerary furnishings without equal in the history of Egyptology.

Inside a tomb of modest proportions and moderate artistic quality in which only the burial chamber was decorated with wall paintings (showing, among other scenes, court dignitaries carrying the king's catafalque), Carter found a priceless hoard of precious objects, furnishings, statues, and other items. These are now displayed in the Egyptian Museum in Cairo, where they occupy a large section of the first floor. Tutankhamun's tomb is the only intact royal burial place to be found in the Valley of the Kings. Scholars assert that even a couple of robberies attempted during the Twenty-first Dynasty caused almost no damage; the tomb was re-sealed and fortunately never again desecrated.

After the burial chamber had been opened, various unfortunate events in the lives of Lord Carnavon (Howard Carter's financial backer) and other members of the archeological mission, led to legends about a 'curse' tied to Tutankhamun and his violated tomb. The real mysteries, however, are both different and more interesting to resolve. First among them are the origin and the exact role of Tutankhamun. He may have been the son of the religious reformer Akhenaten (it must be remembered that the owner of this tomb was born with the name 'Tutankhaten,' or 'living image of Aten'). Aten was of course the one and only god, the solar disc Aten, whose worship Pharaoh Akhenaten had imposed.

Tutankhamun's burial place has been the focus of innumerable studies and publications. Thousands of remains have been recovered from these narrow chambers where they had remained undisturbed for centuries, only for the tomb to be eventually emptied of all its treasures. Tutankhamum's quartzite sarcophagus, still in situ, preserved the pharaoh's mummified body. Unfortunately, it has suffered much damage owing to poorly conceived autopsies by specialists. Two others sarcophagi—one in gold-plated wood, the other in solid gold—together with the gold and lapis lazuli mask placed directly on the mummy are displayed in a special hall of the Egyptian Museum in Cairo. They perpetuate Tutankhamun's memory and remind all visitors of the grandeur of an unrepeatable past.

104-105 THE EXTERNAL MUMMIFORM COFFIN PROTECTING THE MUMMY OF THE PHARAOH IS STILL FOUND INSIDE THE QUARTZITE SARCOPHAGUS.

105 THE CARTOUCHE IS LOCATED ON THE THRONE OF TUTANKHAMUN. BELOW, THE SPLENDID GOLD FUNERAL MASK RECREATING THE FEATURES OF THE YOUNG PHARAOH CAN BE ADMIRED.

106 TOP IN THIS PAINTING, THE NIGHT BOAT OF KHEPRI THAT SAILS FOR SIX HOURS WITH GODS BEARING THE ASPECTS OF A BABOON CAN BE SEEN.

106 BOTTOM PART OF A FUNERAL PROCESSION IS ILLUSTRATED ON THE WALLS OF THE TOMB.

107 TOP FOUR WINGED DIVINITIES PROTECT THE PHARAOH'S MUMMY IN THE QUARTZITE SARCOPHAGUS.

107 BOTTOM TUTANKHAMUN IS GREETED BY THE GODDESS HATHOR WHO OFFERS HIM LIFE, SYMBOLIZED BY THE ANKH.

108-109 AY, TUTANKHAMUN'S SUCCESSOR TO THE THRONE OF EGYPT, OFFICIATES OVER THE RITE OF THE OPENING OF THE MOUTH OF THE PHARAOH SHOWN AS A MUMMY.

H oremheb, a senior official and general at
the time of Akhenaten and his regime
based on his capital city of Akhetaten
(the modern al-Amarna) maintained his
prestigious positions under the reigns of this pharaoh's next
two successors, Tutankhamun and Ay. Then he ascended the
throne himself and ruled Egypt for about 30 years. Not being
of royal descent, like his predecessor Ay, Horemheb, long-
time trusted aid of Tutankhamun, repudiated his first wife and
married Mutnedjmet, sister of Nefertiti. As confirmed by the
lovely statuary group in the Egyptian Museum in Turin, which
portrays them embracing as husband and wife, just like
private citizens, Horemheb's claim to the throne was
legitimated and guaranteed by his wife's royal descent.
Interestingly, the artists who sculptured the monument were
evidently still affected by the 'realistic art' dictates that the
cultural changes of Akhenaten's time had imposed.

Horemheb had already had a tomb prepared for him at
Saqqara, before he became pharaoh. Because of the
plundering of tombs that occurred over the centuries, it was
only recently that Horemheb's tomb was 'rediscovered' and
its exact location positively identified. The initial discovery of
the large burial place with its several decorated rooms
resulted in a transfer of many splendid bas-reliefs to museums
and collections in Bologna, Leiden, and Vienna. By the end of
the process, the tomb was literally a void. The tomb
excavated in the Valley of the Kings introduced a conceptual
and architectural innovation into the Theban area bearing
the mark of Amarna. In other words, the rooms were arranged
in line with the entrance. This style had only one precedent in
the Valley of the West, the more modest burial place of Ay,

OF HOREMHEB

110 TOP THE PHARAOH IS GREETED BY THE GOD WITH THE JACKAL'S HEAD, ANUBIS.

110 BOTTOM HOREMHEB, HERE SHOWN AS SOVEREIGN AND STILL ALIVE, IS EMBRACED BY THE GODDESS HATHOR.

110-111 ON THIS WALL LOCATED ON THE UPPER PART OF THE WELL, THE PHARAOH IS PORTRAYED IN THE ACT OF MAKING OFFERINGS TO SEVERAL GODS: OSIRIS, HATHOR, ISIS, AND HORUS.

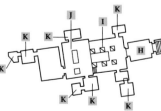

N

LEGEND

A ENTRANCE STAIRWAY
B FIRST DESCENDING CORRIDOR
C SECOND DESCENDING CORRIDOR
D SECOND PASSAGEWAY
E WELL
F FIRST PILLARED ROOM
G THIRD DESCENDING CORRIDOR
H ANTECHAMBER
I SECOND PILLARED ROOM
J FUNERAL CHAMBER
K STOREROOMS

himself also a top official at Amarna and, subsequently, a king of the Eighteenth Dynasty. In addition to the brilliant polichromy of their scenes, the partially unfinished wall decorations reveal the various stages of artistic production from the preparatory drawing to the work of the sculptor. The iconographic and textual repertory is enriched by a new chapter in the royal funerary literature: the appearance of the Book of Gates describing the various obstacles or 'doors' that separate the twelve hours of the night. The Book of Gates thus completes the Book of the Amduat.

THE TOMB OF HOREMHEB

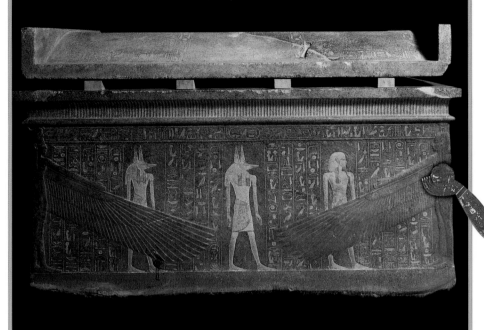

112 THE GODDESS HATHOR, LADY OF THE WEST AND THE SKIES, WEARS AN UNUSUALLY DESIGNED WIG SURMOUNTED BY THE SOLAR DISK HELD BETWEEN HER HORNS.

113 TOP THE RED-GRANITE SARCOPHAGUS IS STILL FOUND IN THE FUNERAL CHAMBER.

113 BOTTOM THE SOLAR BOAT AND THE SOULS OF THE DEAD ARE PORTRAYED IN TWO REGISTERS ON THE WALLS OF THE SECOND PILLARED ROOM, WHERE THE BOOK OF DOORS IS ILLUSTRATED.

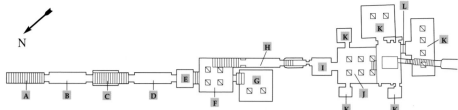

LEGEND	
A Entrance stairway	G Room of the drawings
B First corridor	H Corridor
C Ramp	I Antechamber
D Second corridor	J Funeral chamber
E Well	K Annexes
F Upper pillared room	L Passageway lacking decorations

"On October 16, 1817, I continued my excavations in the valley of Biban el-Moluk and I indicated the very promising spot that compensated for all the hard work that I had been put through during my research. I would like to call this a happy day, perhaps the best of my whole life." So wrote Belzoni in his valuable and fluent Narrative of the Operations and Recent Discoveries within the Pyramids, Temples, Tombs, and Excavations in Egypt and Nubia. The volume was published in 1820, after Belzoni's return to England, and dealt, among much else, with the discovery of Seti I's tomb. This pharaoh had already had prepared a tomb for his father Ramesses I; it can be defined as modest only because of the narrowness of the hastily cut rooms. Then for his own everlasting memory, Seti ordered the excavation of the most beautiful and biggest burial place in the Valley of the Kings. It was modeled on Horemheb's tomb, the first in the Valley whose approach route adhered to a single axis, without a hairpin curve as had been previously used. Seti I had a syrinx cut that penetrated more than 325 feet into the rock.

The burial chamber was reached via steep steps and long corridors. These led initially to a square room in which a well had been dug (later filled up by Belzoni himself) and ended in two large, pillared halls.

In the left-hand corner of the back wall of one of these halls is the entrance to the innermost section of the tomb. Here other stairs and corridors branch off in the same direction but no longer on the same axis as the entry route so far. They lead to the burial chamber with its sarcophagus. Opening off the burial chamber, with its characteristic vaulted ceiling, were a group of rather large rooms intended to contain the funerary furnishings. Belzoni shipped out Seti's enormous aragonite sarcophagus—worthy of a pharaoh whose fame extended far beyond the borders of ancient Egypt. Today, his sarcophagus, an important piece of historical evidence, holds pride of place in Sir John Soane's Museum, London, a magnificent mansion that the distinguished architect and art collector designed, lived in, and in 1835 bequeathed with its contents to the nation.

Belzoni found few other objects in the tomb as it had been robbed more than once in antiquity. Among the items that survived from what were certainly rich and splendid funerary furnishings were a pair of wooden statues of divinities, one with the head of a baboon, the other with the head of a falcon, today in the British Museum. Their specific function is not entirely clear.

THE TOMB OF SETI I

114-115 *THE FOUR COLUMNS IN THE UPPER PILLARED ROOM ARE DECORATED WITH REPRESENTATIONS OF THE PHARAOH IN THE COMPANY OF VARIOUS GODS.*

115 *TOP LEFT* SETI I *IS GREETED BY THE GODDESS HATHOR.*

115 *TOP RIGHT AND BOTTOM* IN *THE PHOTOS, DETAILS TAKEN FROM* THE BOOK OF THE DOORS *CAN BE SEEN, FOUND ON THE WALLS OF THE PILLARED ROOM.*

116 TOP AND 116-117 THE
RIGHT WALL OF THE
ANTECHAMBER IS DECORATED
WITH EXTRAORDINARY
MULTICOLORED BAS-RELIEFS,
WHICH TODAY HAVE
UNFORTUNATELY LOST PART OF
THEIR ORIGINAL COLOR.

116 BOTTOM IN THE DETAIL,
THE FIGURE OF A PRIEST CAN BE
SEEN, RECOGNIZABLE BY HIS SIDE
BRAID.

117 BOTTOM THIS RAM IS
PORTRAYED IN THE
ANTECHAMBER.

118 TOP THE GODDESS NEPHTHYS DOMINATES THE NORTHERN WALL IN THE FUNERAL CHAMBER OF SETI I.

118 BOTTOM ACCOMPANIED BY HORUS, THE PHARAOH SETI I PRESENTS HIMSELF TO OSIRIS.

118-119 THIS VIEW MAKES IT POSSIBLE TO APPRECIATE THE RICHNESS OF THE DECORATIONS IN THE FUNERAL CHAMBER.

119 TOP THESE FIGURES TAKEN FROM THE BOOK OF THE DOORS ARE PORTRAYED ON A WALL IN AN ANNEX.

120 TOP LEFT AND RIGHT A FEW ANNEXES BRANCH OFF FROM THE FUNERAL CHAMBER OF SETI I, FROM WHERE IT IS POSSIBLE TO SEE THE ENTRANCE TO AN UNDERGROUND PASSAGEWAY.

120 BOTTOM AND 121 THESE IMAGES REFER TO VARIOUS FIGURES IN THE BOOK OF THE AMDUAT, A SACRED TEXT FOUND ON THE WALLS OF MANY NEW KINGDOM TOMBS IN THE VALLEY OF THE KINGS. THE BOOK TELLS OF THE NIGHTTIME VOYAGE THAT THE PHARAOH MUST COMPLETE IN THE NETHERWORLD, AND OF ALL THE TESTS THAT THE SOULS OF THE DEAD MUST FACE.

THE TOMB

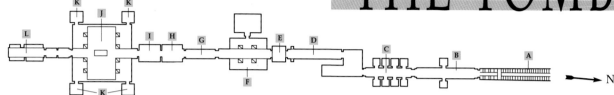

LEGEND		
A ENTRANCE	E WELL	I ANTECHAMBER
B FIRST CORRIDOR WITH TWO ANNEXES	F PILLARED HALL WITH ANNEX	J FUNERAL CHAMBER
C SECOND CORRIDOR WITH EIGHT ANNEXES	G FOURTH CORRIDOR	K SIDE ANNEXES
D THIRD CORRIDOR	H ANTECHAMBER	L REAR ANNEXES

122

OF RAMESSES III

*122 THIS PORTRAIT OF
RAMESSES III, DRESSED UP WITH
A URAEUS AND A WIG, IS FOUND
ON THE SIDE OF A COLUMN IN
THE FIRST PILLARED HALL.*

*123 TOP LEFT MUMMIFORM
GENIES ARE VISIBLE IN THE PHOTO.*

*123 TOP RIGHT THE GOD OF THE
NILE, HAPY, BEARS OFFERINGS
IN THE FORM OF FOODSTUFFS.*

*123 BOTTOM RAMESSES III IS
IMMORTALIZED HERE IN THE ACT
OF OFFERING INCENSE.*

The tomb of Ramesses III (1198-1166 B.C.), one of the last great pharaohs of ancient Egypt, had been noted by Greek travelers such as Strabo. Its first modern visitor was the Scots explorer James Bruce in 1768. The complex, which penetrates the rock for over 400 feet, is among the most majestic of all royal burial sites and has rooms featuring rich and even uncommon decorations and funerary texts, which range from the Litanies of Ra to the Book of the Amduat and the Book of Gates. The access route basically follows the single-axis custom of the Ramesside tombs of the Twentieth Dynasty. However, to avoid intersecting the nearby tomb of Pharaoh Amenmesse (1226-1221B.C.), the route shows a slight deviation from the main axis as it advances to the final corridors and rooms leading on to the burial chamber. The tomb is famous for it exceptional decorations that depict the preparation of foods, the presentation of the offerings, weapons, jewelry, and two harpists who praise the king before the gods Onuris, Shu, and Atum. Ramesses III's pink granite sarcophagus, found in the eight-pillared burial chamber, was sold and is now displayed in the Louvre, while its cover is in the Fitzwilliam Museum, Cambridge, Britain.

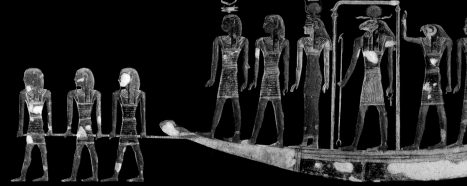

124 TOP *THE PHARAOH, ON THE LEFT, HOLDS A CUP CONTAINING BURNING INCENSE.*

124 BOTTOM *THE SOLAR BOAT CARRIES THE GOD AMUN-RA WITH HIS UNMISTAKABLE RAM'S HEAD ENCIRCLED BY A SOLAR DISK.*

125 TOP *RAMESSES III OFFERS AN IMAGE OF THE GODDESS MAAT.*

125 BOTTOM *TWO GODS, ISIS AND ANUBIS, ARE RECOGNIZABLE IN THESE RELIEFS FROM THE TOMB OF RAMESSES III.*

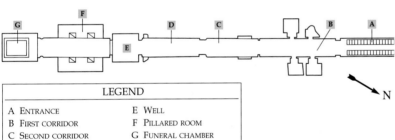

LEGEND

A Entrance	E Well
B First corridor	F Pillared room
C Second corridor	G Funeral chamber
D Third corridor	

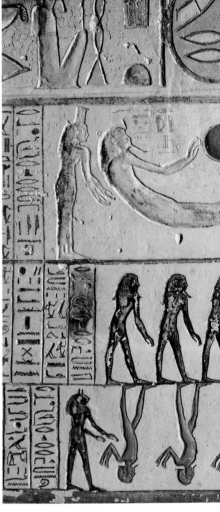

126 top In this scene, the rebirth of the pharaoh is illustrated.

126 bottom The god Amun is often portrayed with the head of a ram.

126-127 In this section of a wall in the tomb of Ramesses IX, cartouches conveying the titles of the king can be seen.

127 bottom The sacred texts, which help the pharaoh to overcome problems in the afterlife, are often accompanied by images of genies and gods.

OF RAMESSES IX

I t can be said that the tomb of Ramesses IX ideally marks the end of the exploration of the royal necropolis of Thebes, just as his death ended the political dominance of Thebes as capital of the New Kingdom. The iconographic repertoire present on the walls of this tomb does not diverge from that of the other Ramesside kings; in fact, it shows many affinities in its style and content with that of Ramesses VI, and the decorations, despite their decay, are still very interesting. In the first two corridors, the texts taken from the Litanies of Ra and a chapter of the Book of the Dead are found, followed by extracts from the Book of Caverns and the Book of the Amduat and illustrations of infernal divinities. The astronomical ceilings and the double representation of Nut on the vault of the burial chamber, together with the steps of the Book of the Day and the Night, recapitulate the life-restoring progression of the sun across the goddess of the sky.

*128 TOP THE WALLS OF THE
FUNEREAL CHAMBER ARE
DECORATED WITH TEXT AND
ILLUSTRATIONS FROM THE BOOKS
OF THE DAY AND THE NIGHT.*

*128-129 AND 129 TOP THE
DECORATIONS ON THE CEILING IN
THIS CORRIDOR RECOUNT THE
NIGHTTIME VOYAGE OF THE SUN
GOD.*

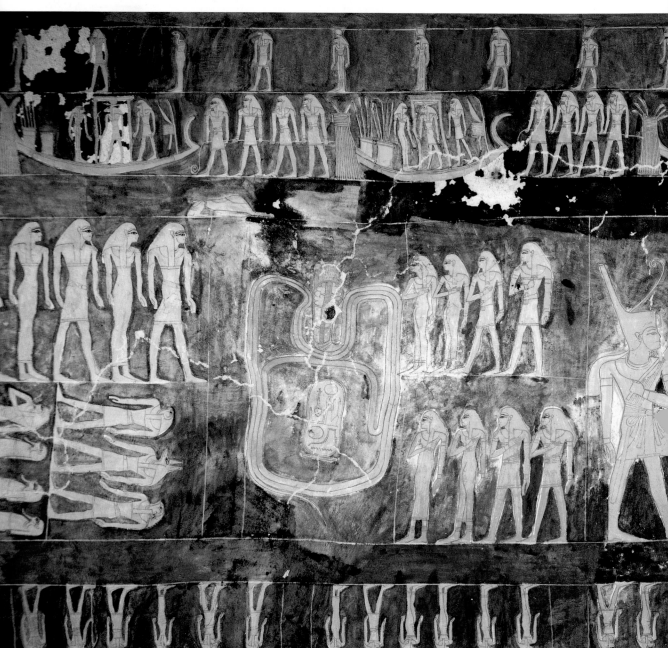

THE TOMB
OF RAMESSES IX

THE VALLEY

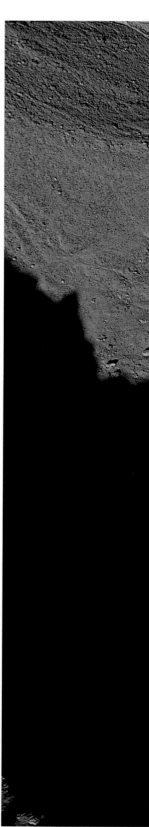

T his valley to the south of the West Theban necropolis, which the ancient Egyptians called ta set neferu ('the place of the children of the king') was the site where the tombs of princes and princesses, along with those of other court dignitaries, were built during the earliest times. It later accommodated mostly the tombs of the queens, or rather the so-called 'royal brides.' Dominated by a natural cave (a symbolic evocation of the bowels of the Celestial Cow, or the goddess Hathor), from which gushed the water that regenerates the dead, the Valley of the Queens contains about 100 burial sites, including simple funerary wells, unfinished tombs, and authentic funerary apartments. Ernesto Schiaparelli, director of the Egyptian Museum in Turin pioneered the archaeological investigation of the valley. Between 1903 and 1906 he discovered some of the most beautiful tombs, including those of Nefertari (wife of Ramesses II) and of the sons of Ramesses III. The French subsequently took over the work of the Italian Archaeological Mission and are still today continuing the study, cleaning, and restoration of all the burial sites in the Valley of the Queens. In the last few years, many interesting finds have been made; they have also generated a series of questions that are at present difficult to give definite answers to. Who, for example, are children of Ramesses III and when were they buried in the Valley of the Queens? The individual who came to the throne as Ramesses VIII must have been among them, but was therefore buried in the Valley of the Kings. The wall paintings of some of the tombs, above all that of Nefertari, are among the most refined in the whole Theban necropolis, both for the quality of their design and for the brilliance of their colors.

130-131 THE AREA THAT CONTAINS THE TOMBS OF THE QUEENS AND SOME PRINCES IS LOCATED IN THE SOUTHERNMOST SECTION OF THE THEBAN NECROPOLISES.

LEGEND
QV55 AMUN-HER-KHEPSHEF
QV66 NEFERTARI

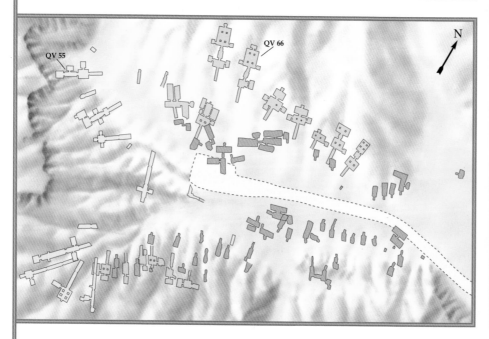

QV 55

QV 66

N

THE TOMB OF

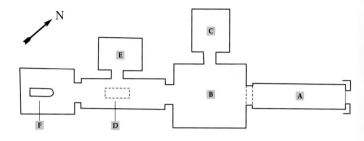

The young crown prince Amun-her-khepshef, son of Ramesses III, who is thought to have died in early adolescence, was buried in one of the most beautiful tombs of the Ramesside period. Simple in structure, with a series of rooms that proceed along the axis of the entrance, consisting of a steep staircase dug out of the earth, the burial place of Amun-her-khepshef contains many bas-reliefs of exquisite manufacture and great chromatic liveliness. The true protagonist of the wall scenes is, however, Ramesses III, intent on presenting his young heir to the various divinities shown thereon. Wall decorations in the chamber containing the sarcophagus show texts and illustrations taken from chapters 145 and 146 of the Book of the Dead, the anthology originally committed to papyrus but often reproduced on the walls of burial chambers, both royal and less distinguished ones. When Ernesto Schiaparelli found Amun-her-khepshef's pink-granite sarcophagus, it had already been opened, the result of its discovery in the first years of the 1900s. It was then moved to Turin to be exhibited in the city's Egyptian Museum. In the small room situated at the end of the internal route, beyond Amun-her-khepshef's burial chamber, Schiaparelli found the skeleton of a fetus, inside a small wooden coffin. It is now preserved in a special shrine.

N

LEGEND	
A RAMP	E INCOMPLETE WEST
B ANTECHAMBER	ANNEX
C WEST ANNEX	F ACCESS TO THE DOMINION
D FUNERAL CHAMBER	OF OSIRIS

132 AMUN-HER-KHEPSHEF WALKS BEHIND HIS FATHER, RAMESSES III, AND HOLDS UP A KHU-FAN MADE OF AN OSTRICH FEATHER.

133 IMSETY, ONE OF HORUS' CHILDREN, WAS THE PROTECTOR — TOGETHER WITH THREE OTHER BROTHERS — OF THE CANOPIC VASES IN WHICH THE INTERIOR ORGANS OF THE DECEASED WERE PRESERVED.

AMUN-HER-KHEPSHEF

OF NEFERTARI

N

efertari, 'Great Bride of the King' Ramesses II, was buried in the richest and most fascinating tomb of the Valley of the Queens. It was discovered in 1904 by Ernesto Schiaparelli, then director of the Egyptian Museum in Turin. The splendor of Nefertari's tomb has no equal among those of the other queens of the era. For this reason, Egyptologists have hypothesized that the queen enjoyed extraordinary status; she was always portrayed in the foreground with Ramesses II, at least until her death, the date and cause of which is unknown. Nefertari is also remembered for another exceptional fact, namely, her portrayal in grandiose proportions in the small temple at Abu Simbel, where she is shown flanking her husband Ramesses II in a celebration of her identification with the sun god. Other records confirm Nefertari's powerful role, showing her active in political life and enjoying important social status, perhaps following the example of her immediate antecedent, Nefertiti, wife of the religious reformer Akhenaten.

134 TOP MAAT TAKES PART IN THE JUDGMENT OF THE DECEASED ALONG WITH OSIRIS AND THOTH.

134 BOTTOM THIS PROFILE OF NEFERTARI IS PROOF OF THE EXTRAORDINARY ABILITIES OF THE TOMB'S DECORATORS.

135 IN THIS VIEW, THE ANTECHAMBER AND PART OF THE FIRST ANNEX CAN BE SEEN.

LEGEND	
A	RAMP
B	DOOR
C	ANTECHAMBER
D	PASSAGE LEADING TO THE ANTECHAMBER
E	ANTECHAMBER
F	ANNEX
G	DOOR
H	INSIDE RAMP
I	DOOR
J	FUNEREAL CHAMBER
K	WEST ANNEX
L	EAST ANNEX
M	ACCESS TO THE DWELLING OF OSIRIS

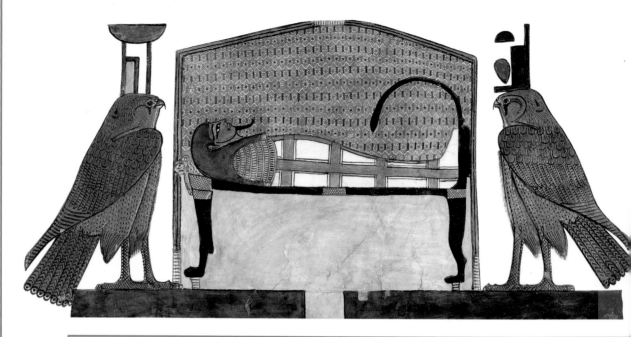

Nefertari's tomb, similar in structure to those of the pharaohs that have been excavated in the Valley of the Kings, presents an admirable example of refined relief-painting on a white background that magnifies both its freshness and liveliness. Most of the iconographic and textual repertoire appears to have been taken from chapters of the Book of the Dead, an authentic synthesis of the eternal cosmogonic ambivalence of Ra-Osiris in ancient Egypt. The book offers the conclusive formula, "Here is Ra who rests in Osiris, here is Osiris who rests in Ra." Among the most famous scenes reproduced on the walls of the burial chamber is one that shows Nefertari playing (between herself and her destiny) senet, a game similar to chess, with the aim of winning otherworldly salvation.

The large burial chamber, its ceiling decorated with astronomic motifs, features four pillars from which stand out Queen Nefertari and large figures of divinities, among them some wearing panther skins. Nefertari's pink-granite sarcophagus originally stood in the center of this room. The few objects in the funerary furnishing (some ushabti, or funerary statues, and a pair of sandals made of palm fiber)

and the fragments of the sarcophagus cover are in the Egyptian Museum in Turin. They were not present in the tomb when it was discovered by Schiaparelli.

During the past decades water infiltration has caused serious damage to Nefertari's tomb and its wall decorations. With expert stabilization and preservation and the restoration of the wall paintings now completed, the tomb has recently been reopened to the public; however, entry is limited to about 100 visitors daily.

138-139 *On a wall of the ramp, the winged goddess Maat and the scorpion goddess Serket are depicted.*

140 *The funereal chamber of Nefertari is characterized by the presence of four pillars.*

141 left *The image refers to the two genies at the doors of the dominion of Osiris.*

141 right *On the northern side of a pillar in the funeral chamber, Osiris appears with his characteristic green skin and royal attributes (a scepter and a flail).*

142-143 *This general photo of the funeral chamber of Nefertari makes it possible to better appreciate the opulent decorative scheme of the tomb.*

141

DEIR AL-MEDINA

The Arab place name Deir al-Medina indicates the ancient settlement encompassing the quarters of the workers and artisans hired to prepare and decorate the tombs in the Valley of the Kings. The rather well-preserved remains of a so-called workers' village were found in a valley close to the Valley of the Queens, below the Theban Peak, the naturally pyramid-shaped mountain that dominates the entire West Theban necropolis. The village is a rare example of an urban framework created by the ancient Egyptians. Already built and enclosed by a bare-brick city wall by the Eighteenth Dynasty, the village consisted of a series of homes mostly built along a main street from which the individual houses were entered. They had a few small rooms and sometimes even a terrace and a dug-out cellar.

Excavations at the site, sponsored by Ernesto Schiaparelli in the early 1900s, soon revealed a considerable mass of documents. These were found partly in the agglomerated remains of the houses, partly in burial places excavated in the adjacent hill, and partly from a now famous deposit in which were stacked thousands of fragments of papyrus or ostraca (limestone flakes). These fragments and ostraca contained inscriptions or sketches by young scribes and artists from throughout the New Kingdom. Thanks largely to the work of the Institut Français d'Archéologie Orientale in Cairo, which early on took over from Schiaparelli's Italian team, the material found at Deir al-Medina has yielded an almost unrivaled reconstruction of Egyptian life and social organization during the period. Thus, in addition to the work routines and complex genealogies, the gossip and small controversies of this limited group of people who lived at Deir al-Medina for about 200 years has come to be known. It is fascinating: scandals, betrayals, and revenge on a union level (the records speak of the first documented 'strike' in history, detailed on a papyrus in the Egyptian Museum in Turn).

The necropolis, dug into the slopes of the western hill of the Deir al-Medina Valley, accommodates a series of beautiful tombs of officials and artisans charge with construction of the royal tombs. The burial places are substantial and almost always richly decorated: a courtyard enclosed by an external wall gives access to a cult chapel, often surmounted by a pyramidion connected to a pyramidal brickwork structure. The burial chambers were reached from the external courtyard or through one of the rooms dug into the hillside. Inside one were found the funerary furnishings of the architect Kha; these were recovered intact and are now exhibited at the Egyptian Museum in Turin; in another the funerary furnishings of Sennedjem, the 'Servant in the House of the Truth;' these items are in the Egyptian Museum in Cairo. The wall paintings in these burial sites usually reflect the religious and ritual repertoire (i.e., illustrations of significant chapters on the preparation of the deceased taken from the Book of the Dead) rather than representations of daily life, as demonstrated by scenes of hunting or working in the fields.

145

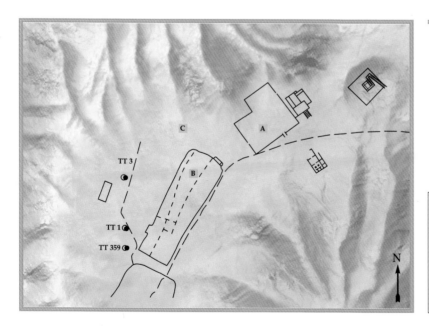

144 THIS AERIAL VIEW MAKES IT POSSIBLE TO APPRECIATE THE SITE OF DEIR AL-MEDINA IN ITS ENTIRETY, WHERE THE WORKERS AND ARTISANS IN THE SERVICE OF THE PHARAOH HAD THEIR LODGINGS AND WERE BURIED.

LEGEND

A PTOLEMAIC TEMPLE
B VILLAGE
C DEIR AL-MEDINA

TT1   TOMB OF SENNEDJEM
TT359 TOMB OF INHERKHAU
TT3   TOMB OF PASHEDU

THE TOMB OF SENNEDJEM

The tomb of Sennedjem, 'Servant in the House of the Truth' (in fact, an official of the necropolis), who lived at the time of Seti I and Ramesses II (Nineteenth Dynasty), was discovered intact by Gaston Maspero in 1886. The rich funerary furnishings, consisting of high-quality furniture and equipment in an excellent state of preservation, can be admired today in the Egyptian Museum in Cairo. The wall decoration of the tomb's single room (the burial chamber), which is open to visitors, is extraordinary for its richness of color and liveliness of design, featuring scenes from a variety of books connected to the ritual of the netherworld and survival in the afterlife. Sennedjem, with his arm linked to that of his wife Inyferti, is often portrayed in the act of worshiping the gods, concentrating on receiving and allocating offerings, playing senet, or working in the fields of Iaru (as required by the doctrines detailed in chapter 110 of the Book of the Dead). Even the chamber's vaulted ceiling is entirely decorated with scenes from the Book of the Dead's funerary repertoire. Noteworthy among them are the Goddess of the Sycamore, Protectress of the Dead, who holds out offerings to Sennedjem and Inyferti, and a representation of the benu, or a blue heron, the hypostasis of the god Ra, prophetic symbol of the phoenix, capable of regenerating itself.

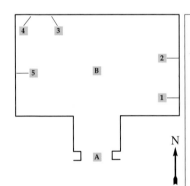

147 TOP THE RITUAL OF THE OPENING OF THE MOUTH CONDUCTED BY A SON OF SENNEDJEM IS ILLUSTRATED ON THE NORTHEAST WALL OF THE TOMB.

147 BOTTOM THE TWO CONSORTS ARE THE MAIN CHARACTERS OF THE RITUAL SCENES, PORTRAYED MAKING AN OFFERING IN THIS PICTURE.

LEGEND
A ENTRANCE
B BURIAL CHAMBER
1 HARVEST SEASON IN PARADISE
2 PLOWING SEASON IN PARADISE
3 OSIRIS BETWEEN TWO *UDJAT* EYES
4 ANUBIS AND THE MUMMY OF THE DECEASED
5 THE DECEASED AND HIS WIFE HONOR SEATED GODS
SENNEDJEM WORSHIPS VARIOUS GODS (CEILING)

N

146 THE SPLENDID TOMB OF SENNEDJEM WAS FOUND ALMOST COMPLETELY INTACT AND IS STILL CONSIDERED EXTRAORDINARY FOR ITS DECORATIVE OPULENCE. ON THE REAR WALL TO THE LEFT, SENNEDJEM CAN BE SEEN WITH HIS CONSORT.

THE TOMB
OF SENNEDJEM

149

148-149 *THE INSIDE OF THE TOMB OF SENNEDJEM IS SEEN HERE FROM THE SOUTHWEST.*

149 *ALONG THE NORTHEAST WALL, THE BLESSED FIELDS OF IARU IN THE NETHERWORLD, AS TOLD IN CHAPTER 110 OF THE BOOK OF THE DEAD, ARE DEPICTED.*

150-151 *ON THE VAULT OF THE FUNERAL CHAMBER, SENNEDJEM IS PORTRAYED WITH HIS WIFE IN VARIOUS MOMENTS OF WORSHIP, EACH DIVIDED INTO ITS OWN PANEL.*

THE TOMB

Inherkhau, 'Foreman of the Lord of the Two Lands in the House of the Truth' in the time of pharaohs Ramesses III and Ramesses IV (Twentieth Dynasty) had the right to a rich tomb of notable artistic quality. The scenes, even though they draw on the customary Book of the Dead and Book of Gates, are rather original if compared with the figurative repertoire in vogue at that time and used for that type of functionary. For example, they portray the procession of the king, queens, and deified princes or the cat of Heliopolis that killed the serpent Apophis. The burial chamber has about thirty scenes. The majority of them can be defined as 'adaptations' of images from the Book of the Dead, with Inherkhau wearing a panther skin typical of the sem-priest or in a linen robe with his wife at his side while he listens to a blind artist perform.

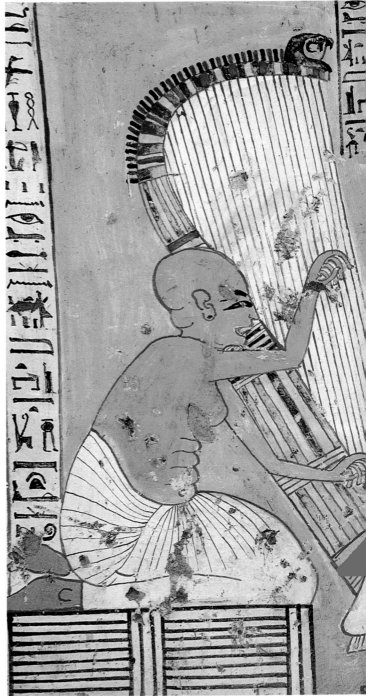

152 The lively decorations in the tomb portray the deceased with various gods and his relatives.

152-153 Inherkhau and his consort are shown seated in front of a blind harpist.

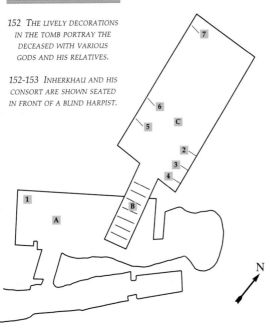

LEGEND

A UPPER HALL	4 THE DECEASED AND HIS WIFE LISTEN TO A BLIND HARPIST
B STAIRWAY	5 THE DECEASED HONORS THE BENU BIRD
C SEPULCHRAL CHAMBER	
1 DECORATED CEILING	6 ANUBIS AND THE MUMMY OF THE DECEASED
2 VENERATION OF A SNAKE	7 A CAT KILLS A SNAKE
3 THE DECEASED RECEIVES OFFERINGS FROM HIS RELATIVES	

N

OF INHERKHAU

153 BOTTOM THE JACKAL-GOD,
ANUBIS, OFFERS A HEART TO THE
MUMMY OF THE DECEASED.

154

154 TOP INHERKHAU,
ACCOMPANIED BY THOTH,
MAKES DONATIONS TO OSIRIS,
LORD OF THE UNDERWORLD.

154-155 INHERKHAU, WITH HIS
WIFE, RECEIVES HIS CHILDREN
AND GRANDCHILDREN AND
ACCEPTS THEIR OFFERINGS.

155 TOP LEFT THE RITE OF THE
KILLING OF THE SERPENT
APOPHIS BY THE CAT OF
HELIOPOLIS SERVED TO WISH
THE DECEASED A SAFE TRIP
THROUGH THE UNDERWORLD.

155 TOP RIGHT INHERKHAU
OFFERS THE GIFTS THAT HAVE
BEEN PLACED ON AN ALTAR TO A
SACRED BENU BIRD.

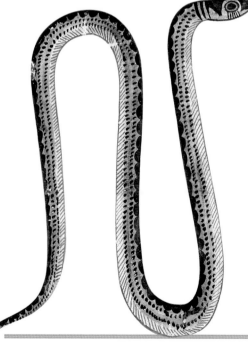

155 BOTTOM IN EGYPTIAN
MYTHOLOGY, THE SNAKE
APOPHIS POSED A DAILY THREAT
TO THE CROSSING OF THE SOLAR
BOAT THAT CARRIED THE DEAD
TO THE AFTERLIFE.

THE TOMB OF PASHEDU

T he tomb of Pashedu, another 'Servant in the House of the Truth' during the Ramesside era, should be noted for the vividly colored decorations that adorn the burial chamber and the narrow vaulted passageway, on the walls of which stand out two big figures of Anubis in the form of a jackal. The deceased and his family are portrayed performing ritual actions, including the symbolic voyage to Abydos, seat of the cult of Osiris, in the act of devotion to the gods, or, in the most prosaic one, quenching their thirst at a stream under a palm tree laden with dates.

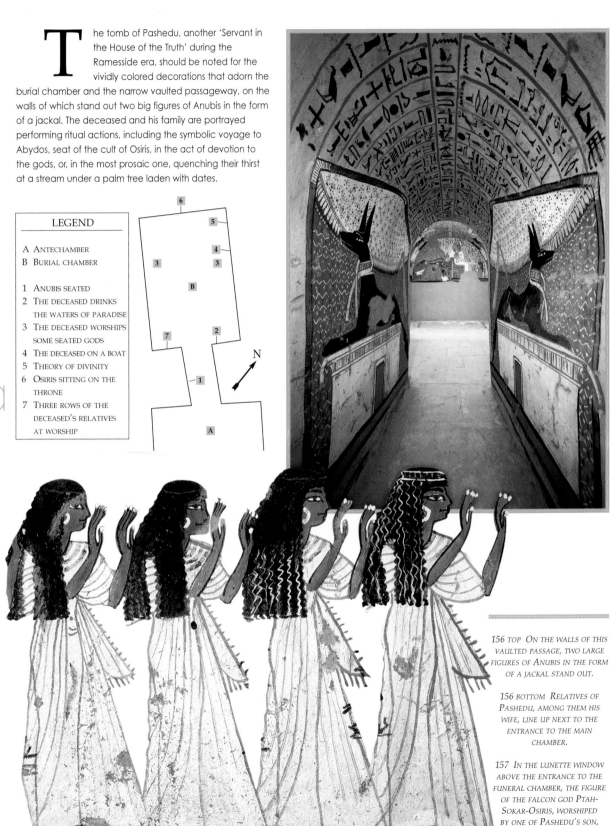

LEGEND

A ANTECHAMBER
B BURIAL CHAMBER

1 ANUBIS SEATED
2 THE DECEASED DRINKS
   THE WATERS OF PARADISE
3 THE DECEASED WORSHIPS
   SOME SEATED GODS
4 THE DECEASED ON A BOAT
5 THEORY OF DIVINITY
6 OSIRIS SITTING ON THE
   THRONE
7 THREE ROWS OF THE
   DECEASED'S RELATIVES
   AT WORSHIP

N

156 TOP ON THE WALLS OF THIS VAULTED PASSAGE, TWO LARGE FIGURES OF ANUBIS IN THE FORM OF A JACKAL STAND OUT.

156 BOTTOM RELATIVES OF PASHEDU, AMONG THEM HIS WIFE, LINE UP NEXT TO THE ENTRANCE TO THE MAIN CHAMBER.

157 IN THE LUNETTE WINDOW ABOVE THE ENTRANCE TO THE FUNERAL CHAMBER, THE FIGURE OF THE FALCON GOD PTAH-SOKAR-OSIRIS, WORSHIPED BY ONE OF PASHEDU'S SON, STANDS OUT.

THE TOMB OF PASHEDU

158 PASHEDU DRINKS THE
WATERS OF PARADISE NEAR A
DATE PALM TO EXTINGUISH THE
FLAMES OF THE UNDERWORLD,
AS PRESCRIBED BY THE BOOK OF
THE DEAD.

159 GODS FROM THE CEILING
(ABOVE). PASHEDU AND HIS
WIFE ARE SEATED ABOARD THE
BOAT THAT WILL BRING THEM TO
THE WEST, TOWARD THE
KINGDOM OF THE DEAD (BELOW).

160-161 IN THIS COMPLEX
SCENE, A FALCON, THE UDJAT
EYE, AND A GOD CARRYING TWO
BRAZIERS APPEAR ALONGSIDE
OSIRIS ON THE THRONE,
TOWERING OVER PASHEDU.

PRIVATE NECROPOLISES

The tombs of functionaries or, as often defined, of private citizens, who lived during the New Kingdom were dug out of valley walls in a vast area in West Thebes. Hundreds of tombs have been discovered, many of which are in good condition and decorated with reliefs or more often with lively paintings. Their locations are now indicated by Arab place names: Dra Abu al-Naga, al-Asasif, Sheikh Abd al-Qurna, al-Khokha, etc.

The tomb entrances are often lost beneath modern villages that sit on top of the ancient necropolises and form a complex tangle of construction, a real headache for archaeologists who, as a result, are forced to limit or even suspend their investigations. The wall paintings, though in many cases unfortunately deteriorated because of problems such as increased humidity, have preserved intact their charm of reproducing in miniature the daily-life activity and atmosphere of over 3000 years ago. In fact, the iconographic repertoire of these private burial places refers only to scenes of 'profane' activities, at times enriched with symbolic values for the afterlife. This is in contrast to the iconographic repertoire of the royal tombs, laden with ritual texts and funerary formulas.

N

LEGEND	
A	DEIR AL-MEDINA
B	SHEIKH ABD AL-QURNA
C	UPPER ENCLOSURE
D	LOWER ENCLOSURE
E	UPPER ENCLOSURE
TT 52	TOMB OF NAKHT
TT 55	TOMB OF MENNA
TT 69	TOMB OF REKHMIRE
TT 96	TOMB OF RAMOSE
TT 100	TOMB OF SENNEFER

162-163 *IN THIS AERIAL VIEW OF THE NECROPOLISES, THE HILLS OF SHEIKH ABD AL-QURNA AND OF AL-KHOKHA CAN BE RECOGNIZED IN THE FOREGROUND. IN THE BACKGROUND, THERE ARE THE CLIFFS THAT FRAME DEIR AL-BAHARI.*

THE TOMB

The tomb of Nakht 'Astronomer-scribe of Amun' under Thutmosis IV (Eighteenth Dynasty), features in its vestibule (its only decorated room) some of the most famous images in Egyptian pictorial art. These include one depicting a banquet with three musicians who entertain the guests by playing their instruments. On the other walls of the tomb appear the more customary scenes of farming life, grape harvesting, winemaking, and hunting and fishing, besides those connected with rituals and offerings.

OF NAKHT

164-165 *NAKHT, ESTEEMED SCRIBE AND ASTRONOMER, STANDS ON A REED BOAT ARMED WITH A STICK (LEFT) AND PRESUMABLY A HARPOON (RIGHT, BUT THE PAINTING WAS NEVER COMPLETED) DURING A HUNTING EXPEDITION ALONG THE BANKS OF THE NILE.*

164 *BOTTOM NAKHT AND HIS WIFE TAUY ARE PORTRAYED IN A POSE OF AFFECTIONATE INTIMACY ON THE WALLS OF THE EAST WING OF THE TRAVERSE HALL.*

165 *BOTTOM THE EAST WING OF THE TRAVERSE HALL PORTRAYS THE TWO SPOUSES IN THE ACT OF OFFERING GIFTS TO THE GODS AND, IN TURN, RECEIVING THEM FROM THEIR RELATIVES.*

166-167 *A HARP PLAYER AND BANQUET GUESTS SING SONGS ABOUT THE TRANSITORY NATURE OF LIFE.*

166 *BOTTOM THE THEME OF THE OFFERINGS IS TAKEN UP IN THIS ILLUSTRATION IN WHICH GIFTS ARE GUARDED BY THE GODDESS OF THE TREE.*

167 *BOTTOM A HARPIST, LUTE PLAYER, AND FLUTIST MOVE SINUOUSLY IN THIS SCENE. THE EXTRAORDINARY ELEGANCE THAT THE ARTIST WAS ABLE TO INFUSE INTO THE COMPOSITION IS WORTHY OF NOTE.*

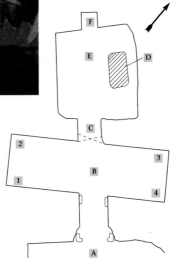

LEGEND

A COURTYARD
B TRANSVERSE REAR HALL
C ENTRANCE TO THE INSIDE HALL
D FUNERAL WELL
E LENGTHWISE INSIDE HALL
F NICHE FOR STATUE

1 OFFERINGS AND FARMING ACTIVITIES
2 SACRED BANQUET
3 FISHING, HUNTING, WINE-MAKING
4 THE DECEASED AND HIS WIFE RECEIVE OFFERINGS

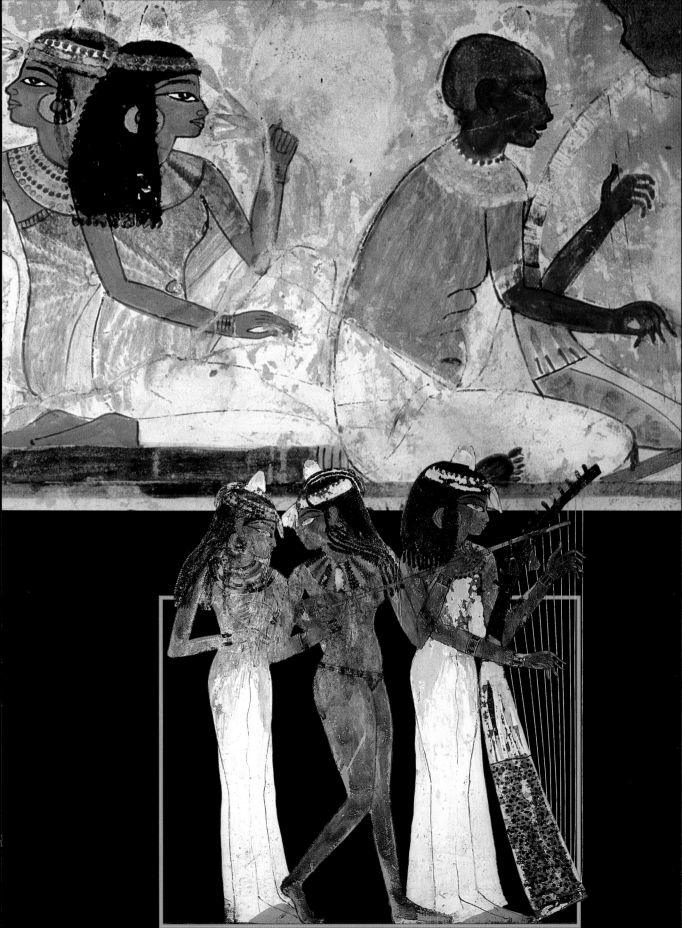

THE TOMB

Very similar in typology and decoration to that of Nakht, the tomb of Menna, 'Scribe of the General Land Office of the Lord of the Two Lands' at the time of Thutmosis IV, is among the most well-known and visited of the whole necropolis. Reusing a more ancient structure, as was common in Egypt, Menna endowed his own burial place with a truly extraordinary and complete repertoire of images, including various nature scenes, all of remarkable artistic quality. They range from farming activities, minutely described in five registers on a wall in the vestibule, to the grandiose scene of hunting and fishing in the swamp, rendered with the most tasteful details of the fauna and relevant actions like the gathering of lotus flowers. Funerary scenes complete the decoration of the tomb, with the appropriate depiction of the ceremony of 'the Opening of the Mouth,' together with Menna and his consort's act of devotion to Osiris, enclosed within his tabernacle.

168

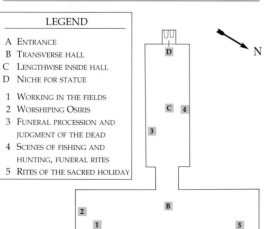

LEGEND

A ENTRANCE
B TRANSVERSE HALL
C LENGTHWISE INSIDE HALL
D NICHE FOR STATUE

1 WORKING IN THE FIELDS
2 WORSHIPING OSIRIS
3 FUNERAL PROCESSION AND
   JUDGMENT OF THE DEAD
4 SCENES OF FISHING AND
   HUNTING, FUNERAL RITES
5 RITES OF THE SACRED HOLIDAY

OF MENNA

168 *Two women are richly dressed and wear wigs on which sits a cone of scented wax.*

168-169 *Accompanied by his family, Menna fishes aboard a bulrush boat.*

169 *bottom Menna's wife, Henut-hauy, is wearing a bright circular earring and a wig on which a cone of scented wax can be seen.*

170 AND 171 THE WALLS OF
THE BURIAL PLACE ARE ADORNED
WITH BUCOLIC SCENES
ILLUSTRATING THE FARMING
CYCLE: PLOWING, PLANTING,
HARVESTING, GATHERING,
REAPING, AND ACTIVITIES
RELATED TO THE APPRAISAL AND
REGISTRATION OF WHEAT.
DIVIDED INTO FOUR REGISTERS,
EACH SCENE DESCRIBED A
SPECIFIC TASK AND A PRECISE
MOMENT IN THE CYCLE.

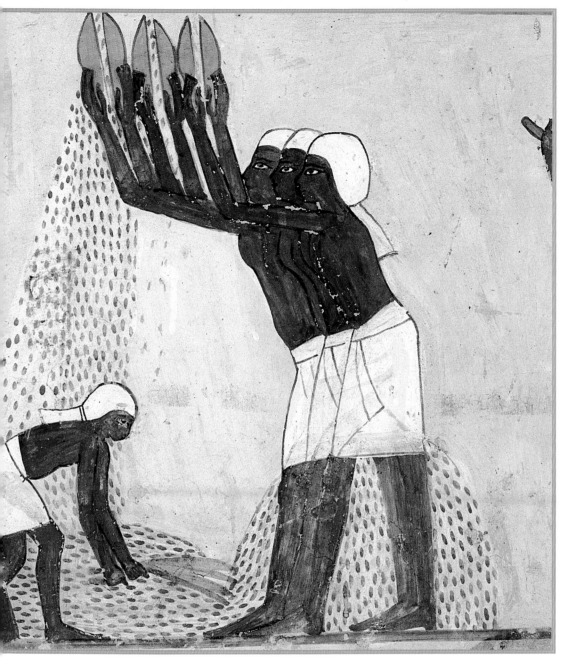

172-173 *MENNA AND HENUT-HAUY, APPEARING AS MUMMIES, ARE THE MAIN CHARACTERS IN THIS CYCLE, WHICH PORTRAYS THEM (TOP) SITTING ON A BOAT ON ITS WAY TOWARD ABYDOS.*

172 BOTTOM *A SCENE FROM THE JUDGMENT OF THE DEAD: THE HEART OF MENNA IS WEIGHED ON A PAN OF A SCALE HELD BY OSIRIS WHILE THE FIGURE OF MAAT, GODDESS OF TRUTH, IS PLACED ON THE OTHER PAN.*

173 TOP ON THE BACK WALL OF
THE WEST WING OF THE
TRANSVERSE HALL, DECORATED
WITH THE AGRICULTURAL CYCLE,
SCENES OF THE VENERATION OF
OSIRIS CAN BE SEEN.

173 BOTTOM TWO OFFERERS
CARRY THE "BOUQUET OF LIFE,"
A BOUQUET OF LOTUS FLOWERS
AND PAPYRUS STEMS, PLANTS
ASSOCIATED WITH REBIRTH AND
PROTECTION RESPECTIVELY.

THE TOMB OF

The tomb of Rekhmire, 'Governor of the City and Vizier' under Thutmosis III and Amenhotep II, is one of the most important in the entire Theban necropolis for its structural dimensions and the nature of its decorations. Rekhmire's elevated rank explains the grandeur of his burial place, which includes a vestibule and a lengthwise oriented chapel with a ceiling that rises 30 feet. The vestibule presents rare and interesting images of the presentation of offerings by foreign peoples. Among these are men from the Land of Punt (roughly Eastern Sudan and Ethiopia) bearing ebony, ivory, leopards, and monkeys; Cretans with vases and golden objects; and black men or Kushites with panther skins, ostrich eggs, monkeys, and even a giraffe. And finally there are Syrians with chariots and weapons in addition to horses, a bear, and a female elephant. The chapel displays on its vast decorated surfaces a complex combination of scenes from daily life that overflows with liveliness and curiosities (many construction and handiwork activities are detailed on these walls), together with illustration of the funeral banquet and other funeral ceremonies. The tendency to transpose in miniature if not actually in draft many of the scenes represented here clearly recalls the tastes and artistic culture of the Middle Kingdom, however achieved in this tomb with more esthetic virtuosity.

REKHMIRE

174-175 *Two women, probably the daughters of Rekhmire, offer sistrums and a* MENAT *necklace to the vizier of Thebes and his consort.*

175 TOP *A group of* NUBIANS *bring gifts typical of their land of origin, among them a giraffe and a monkey.*

175 BOTTOM *The funeral procession is illustrated on the west wall: at the top, the ritual part can be seen; on the bottom, carrying the personal effects of the deceased.*

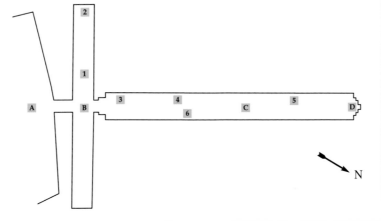

LEGEND

A EXTERNAL COURTYARD
B TRANSVERSE HALL
C PASSAGEWAY
D NICHE

1 THE DECEASED OVERSEES THE COLLECTION OF TAXES FROM UPPER EGYPT
2 TRIBUTES FROM FOREIGN PEOPLES
3 FOOD PREPARATION AND STORAGE
4 ARTISANS, SMITHS, AND BUILDERS AT WORK
5 FUNERAL PROCESSION
6 FUNERAL BANQUET; SCENE OF MUSICIANS

N

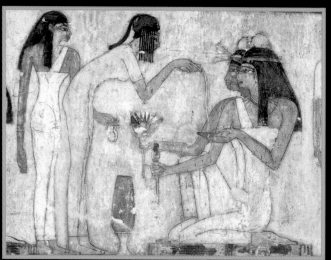

176 TOP A HARPIST PLAYS AND
SINGS AT THE FUNERAL
BANQUET.

176 BOTTOM A SERVANT BOWS
AND POURS BEER FOR THE
CONSORT OF REKHMIRE.

176-177 FLOWER NECKLACES
ARE OFFERED TO A GUEST AT THE
BANQUET, SITTING ON A MAT.

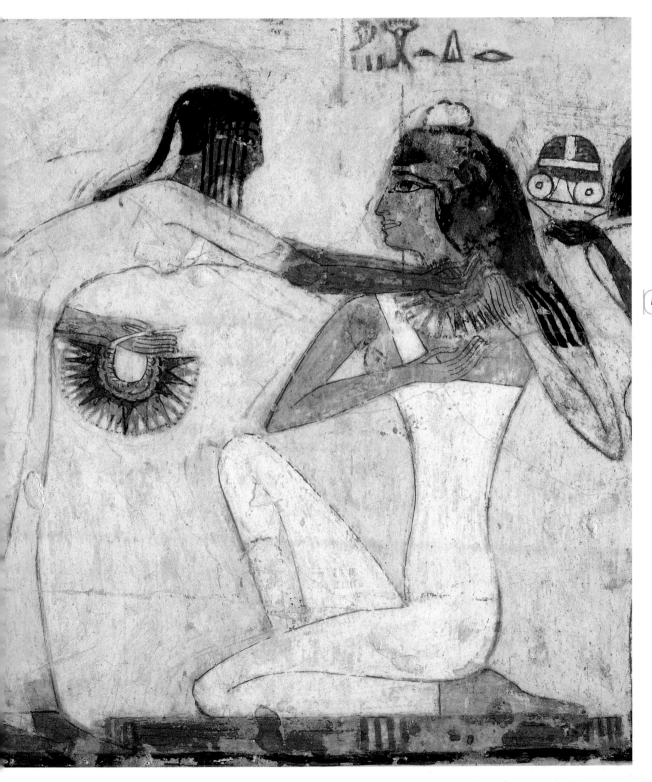

178 BOTTOM SOME OF THE GUESTS AT THE FUNERAL BANQUET IN HONOR OF RAMOSE, VIZIER AND MAYOR OF THEBES DURING THE LAST YEARS OF THE EIGHTEENTH DYNASTY, CAN BE SEEN IN THESE ELEGANT ILLUSTRATIONS.

178-179 THREE SERVANTS WEARING RUFFLED APRONS CARRY OFFERINGS OF WILD GAME AND VARIOUS KINDS OF FRUIT AND FLOWERS TO RAMOSE. THE FIRST ONE HAS BEEN IDENTIFIED AS BEKENAMUN, THE CLOSEST ASSISTANT OF THE VIZIER.

180-181 THE PARENTS OF RAMOSE, NEBY AND APUYA, ARE PORTRAYED HERE WITH EXTRAORDINARY DELICATENESS AND ARTISTIC SENSIBILITY.

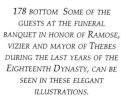

RAMOSE

The tomb of Ramose, 'Governor of the City and Vizier' during the reigns of Amenhotep III and IV, is of particular interest because of its hypostyle hall with bas-relief decorations and wall paintings, which draw on two different stylistic sets of values. One, of perfect quality but by now considered 'affected' because it is too detached from reality, dates back to the art of Amenhotep III's time; the other is decisively more realistic in proportion and adherence to factual evidence, as advocated by the reformer king Amenhotep IV, who later became Akhenaten. The profiles of Ramose and his wife, sculpted in relief on the walls that flank the entrance, are indeed of a rare elegance, just as the scenes of a funeral procession painted on the left wall are of a high artistic level. However, it is the 'Amarnian' reliefs (those influenced by the artistic style of Akhenaten's years), that arouse the most interest. In this case, the pharaoh and queen themselves appear, peeping out from the so-called 'Window of Appearances,' in the context of a presentation of tributes at which Ramose (the deceased) is also present. It must be said, however, that this burial place almost certainly did not accommodate his mummy; he decided to follow his pharaoh to Amarna (as also suggested by the fact that the most recent of the tomb reliefs seem to be unfinished).

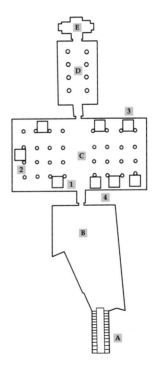

N

LEGEND

A STAIRWAY WITH CENTRAL RAMP
B EXTERNAL COURTYARD
C TRANSVERSE HALL
D LENGTHWISE HALL
E INTERNAL SHRINE

1 FUNERAL BANQUET
2 FUNERAL PROCESSION
3 RAMOSE IS PRAISED AND RECEIVES FOREIGN DELEGATIONS AND FLOWER WREATHES FROM THE TEMPLE
4 THREE YOUNG GIRLS WITH SISTRUMS BEFORE THE DECEASED AND HIS WIFE

182 TOP THE TRANSVERSE
HYPOSTYLE HALL IS THE ONLY
ROOM IN THE TOMB TO HAVE
BEEN DECORATED.

182 BOTTOM THE PHOTO SHOWS
SOME SKETCHES DEPICTING
DEFEATED ENEMIES.

183 TOP A GROUP OF MOURNERS
DEMONSTRATE THE PAIN CAUSED
BY THE DEATH OF RAMOSE IN AN
OBVIOUS WAY.

183 BOTTOM THE SERVANTS
CARRY OBJECTS THAT WILL BE
NEEDED BY RAMOSE IN THE
AFTERLIFE.

THE TOMB OF SENNEFER

The tomb of Sennefer, 'Mayor of the City' at the time of Amenhotep II, is among the most splendid examples of Egyptian pictorial art for the refinement of its forms and the liveliness of its colors. The vast, four-pillared burial chamber is preceded by an antechamber decorated with scenes of offerings being made to the deceased and adoration being paid to the gods. Extraordinary for its content and the excellent state of preservation of its paintings, the tomb of Sennefer is notable above all for its ceiling. This is decorated with bunches of grapes that skillfully take advantage of the irregularity of the internal area, almost seeming to be a real arbor perceivable in its three-dimensional form. The tomb also has customary scenes from the funerary ritual, showing priests employed to proceed with the 'Opening of the Mouth' ceremony. There are also summaries from key chapters of the Book of the Dead, which are recalled elsewhere in the tomb through illustrations or specific allusions, such as 'Go out at day to see the light again' exhortation rendered symbolically by the burial chamber itself.

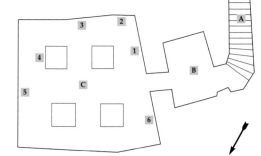

LEGEND

A	Stairway	3	Scenes from the Book of the Dead
B	Antechamber		
C	Burial chamber	4	Priests making offerings
1	Sennefer and Meryt	5	Pilgrimage to Abydos
2	Purification ceremony	6	Meryt and Sennefer

N

184 LEFT MERYT OFFERS A DRINK TO SENNEFER, AMENHOTEP'S CHANCELLOR WHILE HE WAS ALIVE.

184 RIGHT SENNEFER SITS WITH HIS WIFE MERYT NEAR AN ISHED TREE, A SYMBOL OF ETERNAL LIFE.

185 THE SUPERINTENDENT OF THE GARDENS OF AMUN, SENNEFER DESERVED A BURIAL PLACE FEATURING A MASS OF FLORAL DECORATIONS.

186-187 THE FUNEREAL CHAMBER IS FULL OF DECORATIONS PORTRAYING SCENES CONNECTED WITH LIFE AND HAPPINESS.

INDEX

PHOTO CREDITS

192 IN THE PAINTINGS
ADORNING THE VAULT OF HIS
BURIAL CHAMBER, SENNEDJEM
OFTEN APPEARS WITH HIS WIFE
IN THE ACT OF HONORING THE
GODS OF THE HEREAFTER.

COVER
THE TEMPLE OF LUXOR.
PHOTOGRAPH BY
MARCELLO BERTINETTI/
ARCHIVIO WHITE STAR

BACK COVER
CLOCKWISE FROM TOP LEFT:
AERIAL VIEW OF THE
TEMPLE OF KARNAK.
PHOTOGRAPH BY
MARCELLO BERTINETTI/
ARCHIVIO WHITE STAR

THE TOMB OF SENNEFER.
PHOTOGRAPH BY
ARALDO DE LUCA/
ARCHIVIO WHITE STAR

PROFILE OF NEFERTARI FROM
THE QUEEN'S TOMB.
PHOTOGRAPH BY
ARALDO DE LUCA/
ARCHIVIO WHITE STAR

CLOSE-UP OF A COLOSSUS
OF RAMESSES II FROM THE
TEMPLE OF LUXOR.
PHOTOGRAPH BY
ALFIO GAROZZO/
ARCHIVIO WHITE STAR